W9-BUE-673

SMALL GROUP IDEA BOOK

Resources to Enrich

- ☐ Community
- ☐ Worship
- ☐ Prayer
- ☐ Nurture
- ☐ Outreach

CINDY BUNCH, EDITOR

InterVarsity Press
Downers Grove, Illinois

InterVarsity Press® is the book-publishing division of InterVarsity Christian Fellowship®, a student movement active on campus at hundreds of universities, colleges and schools of nursing in the United States of America, and a member movement of the International Fellowship of Evangelical Students. For information about local and regional activities, write Public Relations Dept., InterVarsity Christian Fellowship, 6400 Schroeder Rd., P.O. Box 7895, Madison, WI 53707-7895.

Cover illustration: Roberta Polfus
ISBN 0-8308-1167-2

Printed in the United States of America ♾

Library of Congress Cataloging-in-Publication Data

Small group idea book: resources for community, worship and prayer, nurture and outreach/Cindy Bunch, editor.
p. cm.
ISBN 0-8308-1167-2 (paper: alk. paper)
1. Church group work. I. Bunch, Cindy.
BV652.2.S57 1996
253'.7—dc20 *95-26751*
CIP

---

17 16 15 14 13 12 11 10 9 8 7 6 5 4 3 2 1
10 09 08 07 06 05 04 03 02 01 00 99 98 97 96

Introduction

In 1982 a small group of InterVarsity Christian Fellowship (IVCF) staff workers (Steve Barker, Judy Johnson, Jimmy Long, Rob Malone and Ron Nicholas, coordinator) created *Small Group Leaders' Handbook.* Used by a variety of groups including prison ministries and Officers' Christian Fellowship, that groundbreaking book was of great service to both the campus and the church.

In 1995 another team (Jimmy Long, coordinator, Ann Beyerlein, Sara Keiper, Patty Pell, Nina Thiel and Doug Whallon) wrote a new handbook, called *Small Group Leaders' Handbook: The Next Generation,* which I edited. In the process of writing that book we found that one of the most valued features of the original book was the resource section. We decided that there was enough helpful material available to create a separate book of resources. Thus the *Small Group Idea Book* was born.

This book is a collaborative effort. We included ideas from small group specialists as well as InterVarsity staff and students from across the country. To give an idea of the broad national support from contributors, we listed the abbreviation of their states after their names on the first reference. We particularly want to thank the Downstate Illinois team who submitted the most ideas of any IVCF area and won a pizza party. Runners up included Central/South New Jersey and Western Washington. Many ideas from the original resource section of *Small Group Leaders' Handbook,* compiled by Judy Johnson, are here as well.

There are four sections which represent the four key components of a small group: community, worship and prayer, nurture, and outreach. Ideas within each section are organized alphabetically. Using a mix of ideas from each of these four sections will help group members to grow in relationship to God and to one another.

Some of the sections are subdivided to make them more useful. In chapter one, "Community Resources," we have provided ideas that are appropriate for any phase of a group's life. You'll find ideas for the first few meetings of a small group, ideas for the start-up phase as people continue to question what the group is and whether they want to be a part of it, ideas for the shake-up or conflict phase when the honeymoon is over and group ownership is established, ideas for the live-it-up or action phase when real community is taking place and people are growing, and ideas for the wrap-up phase when the group disbands and needs celebration and closure. Outreach is divided into three key areas: reaching seekers, world mission, and social awareness and action.

We plan to expand and update this book as needed, so if you have ideas you would like to submit for a future edition, feel free to send them to me at InterVarsity Press, P.O. Box 1400, Downers Grove, IL 60515. I can be reached via e-mail at cbunch@ivpress.com. (By submitting an idea you are granting InterVarsity Press permission to reprint your idea. If we use your idea and have a correct mailing address, we will send you a copy of the new edition.) You may also be interested in my column, "The Small Group Doctor," on our Web site at http://www.gospelcom.net/ivpress. If you want more information on the phases of small groups, see the *Small Group Leaders' Handbook: The Next Generation* or *The Big Book on Small Groups.* I'd love to receive letters from you describing how you have used these ideas in your group.

In a world of isolation and fragmentation small groups are a powerful way for people to connect with one another and experience the power of the gospel. May God bless your small group ministry.

Cindy Bunch

1
COMMUNITY RESOURCES

Well, I haven't actually *died* to sin, but I did feel kind of faint once!

To help make this chapter useful we've divided the activities according to the phases of group life. Additionally, some activities are grouped by the length of time they require. This should help you pick the right activity for your needs.

Activities for any phase of a group's life

These ideas are designed to help you "check in" with each other about how you're doing, encourage each other and enjoy being together.

■ *Affirmation exercise* by Ann Beyerlein, Ill. Write each person's name on the top of a sheet of paper. Pass the pages around the group and write words of affirmation and encouragement on each person's page. Use these pages to thank God for each other.

■ *Care packages* by Sue Sage, Wash. Put these together for each other during a stressful time—finals, end of summer, holidays. Some things to include are fruit, aspirin, cough drops, blue books and #2 pencils, crazy stress relief toys like those bouncy balls, cookies, granola bars, tea . . . anything that is conducive to study or stress relief.

■ *E-mail encouragement* by Amy Brooke, Ind. Break the group up into partners who will e-mail each other regularly to challenge one another to keep up with quiet times and Bible study. Talk about what God is teaching you between small groups or as you reflect on the small group meeting.

■ *Found collage* by Irma Hider, Ill. Give each member five minutes to go outside and collect garbage. These have to be things that aren't useful anymore—a dead flower, rocks, bottle caps, paper bags, flyers. They can't buy anything. If done at a first, second or third meeting, each member has to make something that describes themselves using all of the garbage he or she collected. If done for a closing meeting, have each member pick someone else's name out of a hat and make something that reflects the other person, something they appreciated about them or something they see them doing in the future. Or instead of going out and looking for garbage, the leader can bring miscellaneous materials like Q-

Tips, cotton balls, construction paper, paper plates, crayons, tacks, popsickle sticks, bottle caps, Pringles cans, balloons, paper cups or paper clips.

■ *Informal gatherings* by University of Illinois campus staff. You will want to spend some time together in informal settings. These will help you be more comfortable with each other and help you appreciate people in different settings. Some possibilities are to:

☐ go out to eat or have a cafeteria meal together
☐ make popcorn, ice cream or pizza
☐ play volleyball, football, softball or soccer
☐ make a meal together or have a cookout
☐ plan a retreat in which you can incorporate many activities
☐ read a fun story—*Winnie the Pooh, The Velveteen Rabbit,* a Dr. Seuss book
☐ play games like the Ungame, Scattegories, Pictionary or Trivial Pursuit
☐ read a play aloud together, each taking a different role—there are many good ones in *A Man Born to Be King*. It's good nurture too!
☐ go on a hike; fly a kite
☐ do laundry together
☐ watch a movie
☐ go ice skating, rollerblading or bowling
☐ visit each other's churches (if applicable)
☐ greet people at large group or at church Sunday morning
☐ go on a road trip to visit each other's families, other fellowships or an inner-city ministry
☐ do something with another small group (challenge them to a volleyball game, Pictionary tournament, etc.)
☐ go see a play, concert or athletic event that one of your group members is participating in.

■ *Passing the peace.* At the end of a meeting, especially when you've had significant personal discussion, you may want to gather in a circle, join hands and pass the words of the benediction around the group—"May the peace of Christ go with you, Jim." The recipient will respond, "And also with you, Mary."

■ *Postcards from home* by Amy Brooke. Before a break in your meetings for holidays or the summer bring in 3 × 5 "postcards" and have each person write to the group about their ideal break. Mix them up and let people read someone else's to the group. Use this as a launching point to talk about expectations and concerns prior to break.

■ *Purchasing pairs* by Irma Hider. This is a good activity to help prayer partners get to know each other. The leader gives each *pair* one or two dollars to spend. They are to buy something for the whole group and bring it to the next meeting. When done early in the year, it encourages people to return to small group to report. If done later in the year, when group members know each other, have the pairs buy things that are characteristic of certain members. For example, Carrie gets a Band-Aid because she is great at helping others. Mark gets chocolate with almonds because he is sweet and nutty.

■ *A round.* A round is when you give each member in the group thirty seconds to tell how he or she is feeling right now. (Go in a circle.) It may be used at the beginning of any group session or at the end. It is designed to be a short status report. No feedback or evaluation of one another is allowed. After everyone has shared, the group has the option of following up or asking clarification of a group member. A short quick round may do several things:

□ Members become more aware of their feelings.

□ They learn to report feelings (emotions) without evaluation.

□ Hidden agendas that may otherwise hinder the group process may be brought out into the open, or unfinished business at the end of a meeting may be discovered.

□ It can help people open up during the shake-up stage.

You can adapt the round by having everyone report their feelings in weather terminology—partly cloudy, sunny and so on. This is helpful for people who have trouble using feeling words.

■ *The spiritual athlete* by L. Choi and M. Wang, Ill. Having group members take this assessment of their spiritual health (revealing as much detail as they wish) gives the small group leader a clue as to how to minister to the group.

Check all symptoms that apply:

_____ Achilles heel (a perpetual sin)
_____ Headaches
_____ Healthy
_____ Heartaches
_____ Hungry for meat
_____ Lame-footed
_____ Need a coach
_____ Need encouragement
_____ Off the path
_____ On crutches
_____ Overanxious
_____ Overfed and under-exercised
_____ Starving
_____ Tendinitis
_____ Tunnel vision
_____ Underchallenged
_____ Weary
_____ Other: _______________

Type of Runner (Which are you?)

_____ Loner
_____ Pack runner (need constant support to stay on track)
_____ Running in circles (lacking vision)
_____ Sprinter (strong for a while; need to grow in endurance)
_____ Strong and even-paced (steadily making progress; welcome a challenge)

Road of the Saints (Where are you?)

_____ Waiting to start
_____ Newborn
_____ Toddler
_____ Adolescent
_____ Young adult
_____ Mentor

What I want to accomplish by the end of the year:

Needs I have right now:

Ideas for the first few meetings

These are get-acquainted games and discussions to help you break the ice. Many are brief, so you may want to use several. Some of these ideas are active and may seem silly to group members, but acting goofy can help people feel more relaxed. These ideas will be helpful for you for the first three to six meetings, but after that you'll want to move on to activities that will take you deeper.

■ *Appointments* by Tom Sirinides, N.J. Hand out sheets of paper. Draw lines to make four sections. Number the areas one through four. Now make appointments with four different people. Once everyone has four different people's names written down, the leader calls, "Number one!" and everyone gets together with the first appointment. Introduce yourselves, ask each other about your day or week. In a little while, the leader calls, "Number two!" and so on until all the appointments have been completed. You can have people set up more or fewer than four appointments depending on the time available. Allow five to ten minutes per appointment.

■ *Bag skits* by Tom Sirinides. Before people arrive, get two or three shopping bags, one bag for every team you'll have. Put five to ten random items from around your house (or dorm room) in each bag. The things in each bag should be different from those in the others. It doesn't really matter what items you choose; be creative or dull. When people arrive, divide into teams, one team for each bag you have. Give each group a bag. They have ten minutes (or some such time) to create a skit using all the objects in their bag and every person in their group.

■ *Be an Oreo* by Priscilla Luming, Ill. Buy a bag of Oreo cookies. Go around the circle and tell and demonstrate how you go about eating an Oreo. Then share how your style of eating reflects your personality. For example, "I take the cookie apart, making sure the inside cream is intact and the outside cookies are clean. I eat the inside first, then the cookie parts. This shows that I am particular about how things are done—chronologically and orderly."

■ *The commons game* by Dave Suryk, Ill. Go around the circle and take five minutes to see how many somewhat interesting things everyone has in common (all are left-handed, no one ever wore braces, and so on). Things like "we have feet" don't count.

■ *Fictionary* by University of Illinois staff. One member finds a word in the dictionary that they think nobody knows and reads the word to the group. While he/she writes the real definition on a sheet of paper, the other members make up definitions for the word, write them down and hand them in. The first member reads through the definitions and people vote on which definition they think is the real one. One point is given to each person who guessed the right definition, and one point to the person who made up the definition that received the most votes. Game continues until all members have had a chance to find a word.

■ *Forming groups* by Tom Sirinides. This is a way to form random groups for a game or activity. Take one shoe from everyone, mix them up in a pile and divide the pile into the number of groups you want. People look for their shoes and thus find their groups.

■ *Gimme gimme* by Tom Sirinides. Divide into two or more teams and one leader (who is not on any team). The leader stands at the front of the room and says, "Gimme gimme . . ." (as in "Give me, give me . . .") and then mentions something. Each team then races to give the leader that thing; the first team to do so gets a point. Be creative in what you ask for—a certain type of shoelace, a Bible verse, a song being sung (maybe in a language other than English!) or some sort of exercise or action.

■ *Goofy bowling* by Sue Sage. Each member needs to bring five dollars and a good sense of humor to this event. Pair up and go to any thrift store. Each member "trusts" the other member of their pair to dress them for five dollars or under. Then go bowling as a group in your getups. Be sure to bring a camera, because this is great material for an end of the year slide show.

■ *Hand stomp* by Allen Lincoln, Ohio. Everyone kneels forward on their hands in a circle. Each person puts their left hand to the left of the person's on their left—thus there is someone else's hand placed between your own.

Game begins with someone "stomping" their hand on the ground. Going counterclockwise, the next hand stomps, moving around the circle. One stomp continues the direction. Two stomps reverses the direction. A hand is "taken out of the game" if it stomps out of order.

The game can get fast and furious with both hands involved in the game and reversals possible at any time! Game ends when only one person is left or two people agree to a tie.

■ *Knots* by University of Illinois staff. Everyone puts their hands into the middle of the circle and takes the hands of two others (not next to them). Try to untangle yourselves.

■ *Name that face* by Tom Sirinides. Split into two groups. Have a blanket held up between the two groups so that they cannot see each other. Each team positions one person facing the center of the blanket. On the count of three, the blanket is dropped, and the two people are suddenly facing each other. The first one to call out the other one's name "wins." Repeat the process. (It's one way to learn names!)

■ *The no-gift game* by Sue Sage. This is a great Christmastime game. You need one pair of dice and two wrapped gifts for every ten people who are at the party. The gifts are best if they are inexpensive and of the white elephant variety. Everyone sits in a circle with the gifts in the middle. Give people the pairs of dice. Set a timer for five minutes and let the fun begin.

Each person rolls the dice hoping for doubles. When someone gets doubles they run to the middle and get a gift out of the center. (Roll the dice only once, and then pass them on.) When there are no gifts left in the center you can take a gift from someone else. At the end of five minutes whoever has the gifts can keep them and must unwrap their treasure so that everyone can see what the ruckus was all about.

■ *Quiz game* by Bill Fader, Mich. Have each person in the group tell their name, hometown, major, number of siblings, favorite subject and any other tidbits of information you'd like to include. Then divide into two groups. The small group leader will call out the name of a person and an info tidbit ("What is Sally's favorite subject?"). The other team has time to confer (three seconds) and give the answer. Score is kept.

This game could also be done in pairs with partners reporting back to the group to give each other's personal history.

■ *Significant clothing* by Priscilla Luming. Have people sit in a circle and share the significance of an item of clothing (or anything they're wearing—a watch, jewelry) that tells about themselves.

■ *Storytelling* by Bill Fader. The small group leader comes up with a list of eight words or so. This list is given to the members, who are working in pairs. Each pair works together to develop a story using those words and then presents them to the group.

■ *Surprise guest* by Tom Sirinides. Each person puts their name on a slip of paper. Drop these in a hat and let each person draw one out. Don't tell whose name you have gotten, but during the next week, you must visit that person. If you see them without trying to do so (for example, in the dining hall), you fulfill your "obligation" only if you actually talk with them for thirty minutes or more.

A variation on this is to eliminate the surprise factor and just have people set up meal or other appointments right then and there for the week ahead.

■ *Two truths and a lie.* Tell two things about yourself which are true and one which is a lie. Everyone tries to guess which one is not true.

Ideas for start-up

These ideas are for groups in the early phase of life. Start-up (or exploration) is the honeymoon period for groups. Some of these may work for you during the shake-up (or conflict) phase as well.

Five- to Fifteen-Minute Activities

■ *Beautiful babies* by Priscilla Luming. Make "baseball cards" out of baby pictures of people in your small group. Each person writes important facts on them like birthplace, your full name, the name if you would have been born the opposite sex. Enjoy passing them around to one another.

■ *Best friend* by Tom Sirinides. Ask each person to describe their best friend. (A variation is for them to describe their favorite family member.)

■ *Community craps* by Shawn Young, Nev. Bring a pair of dice and take turns rolling. According to the numbers you roll, do or answer the following:

2. What movie/TV character are you most like?
3. The person three places to the left may ask you two questions.
4. What do people of the opposite sex like about you?
5. Who has been the biggest influence on you?
6. Ask a question of anyone you choose.
7. What was the best moment of your life?
8. What three words would you use to describe God?
9. Sing at least nine words of your favorite song.
10. Finish this sentence: "I hate it when . . ."
11. Of all the people in the room, who do you have the *least* in common with? Treat that person to lunch this week. (Make an appointment with them before you leave today.)
12. Do all the stupid-human tricks you know.

■ *Dreaming* by Stephanie Moser, Kans. If there were no limits put on time, talent or training, no obstacles in the way, what would you do for God?

■ *Do you believe?* by University of Illinois staff. Give everyone ten pennies (or M&Ms). Let each person have a chance to say something he/she has done that he/she doesn't believe anyone else has done. Everyone who has done it must give that person a penny. The game continues until someone runs out of pennies.

■ *Fill in the blank (sort of)* by Scott Hotaling, Ill. Everyone thinks of a way to fill in the sentence: "I used to ________, but now I just ________." Then, one person begins and completes the first half of the sentence, and the next person completes the second half in the way he or she had planned. The second person then says the first part of the sentence and the third person finishes it. This continues until each person contributes.

■ *The friendship factor* by Nairy Ohanian, Mass. This activity explores attributes of friendships and helps members share their history of friends. Leaders bring white paper and crayons. Take a few minutes to have each member draw a picture of their closest friend back home. This does not need to be artistic, just have fun. Include features that are unique to him or her. Then write two characteristics you appreciate most about this friend. Discuss the pictures and the characteristics of good friendships. Notice the traits that members really desire in friends and work at nurturing those qualities in the group.

■ *Guess who?* by Tom Sirinides. Everyone writes a sentence about themselves, then crumples their paper up and throws it into the middle of the circle. Each person then picks one up. One person opens his or hers and reads it. The group then tries to decide whose it might be. Even the person whose it actually is can participate in the discussion—don't lie, but don't give yourself away either. Continue one by one until all the papers are opened. An added challenge is that no one reveals the true answers until all have been opened and assigned. The group may want to change some previous guesses as the new papers are opened up.

■ *Heroes* by Tom Sirinides. Ask, "Who was your hero as a child?" Or "Who was your favorite TV character as a child?" Or ask about favorite cartoon characters.

■ *"I didn't know that"* by Dave Ivaska, Ill. Tell the group something about yourself that they'd never think to ask you about.

■ *I've never* by Tom Sirinides. Give each person ten beans (or ten pennies, or just have them hold up their ten fingers!). The first player makes a statement like "I've never seen the ocean" or "I've never left this country." (It *must* be a true statement.) Any player who *has* done that thing (that is, seen the ocean, left the country) loses one bean or penny or puts down one finger. Continue around the circle until only one person has any beans, pennies or raised fingers left.

■ *Impact* by Tom Sirinides. Ask each person to tell about someone who has had a significant impact on his or her life (for good, for bad, in whatever area they choose).

■ *Just save one* by Tom Sirinides. Pass around a bowl of colored candies (M&Ms, Reeses' Pieces, Skittles). Tell people to eat as many as they want, but to save *one* piece. After everyone has only one piece, announce a "question to answer" for each color. For example:

red—A happy day in your life
green—Someplace you'd like to visit and why

yellow—Someone you'd like to meet and why
orange—Three traits you'd like in a spouse
brown—A movie you enjoyed and why

■ *Let's celebrate!* by Nairy Ohanian. This activity allows internationals to reconnect with home and exposes group members to each other's cultural traditions. Each person should describe their favorite spiritual or cultural holiday, its purpose, how it is celebrated, how your family celebrates it, and why it is your favorite. Try to connect each holiday to your country's holiday or tradition. Allow members to ask questions of each other.

■ *More than a word* by Tom Sirinides. Each person answers the question "When, if ever, did God become more than a word to you?"

■ *My life's a pipe cleaner* by Tom Sirinides. Hand out pipe cleaners. Each person bends theirs to tell something about their break, or their week, or how they are feeling right now. (Think up your own ideas.)

■ *One day* by Tom Sirinides. Each person answers the question "If you could relive one day of your life, which day would it be?" Or "If you could have one day off unexpectedly, how would you spend it?"

■ *Picture this* by Tiffany Stack, Tenn. Cut out a variety of pictures from old magazines, catalogs or newspapers. Lay them in the center of the group, and ask group members to choose three pictures which they can use to describe themselves. Then have people tell the group how the pictures describe them.

■ *Pockets* by Tom Sirinides. Each person shows the group (and talks about) three things from his or her pockets, wallet, backpack or purse that tell something about him or her.

■ *Proverbs* by Tom Sirinides. Have everyone share a proverb from his or her home country. (This one works best with internationals.)

■ *Silent auction* adapted from Serendipity by Al Hsu, Ill. In silence, jot down in the left margin the dollar amount you bid on each item. The total amount you can bid for all items cannot exceed $1,000. When you open the bids, write the winner's name after each item.

______ Pay off all loans
______ New personal computer with laser printer, CD-ROM, modem and unlimited Internet access
______ Season tickets for sports team of your choice
______ Lunch with the U.S. president
______ Internship at a Fortune 500 company
______ Opportunity to participate in the next Olympics
______ Date with the person of your dreams
______ Lifetime tickets to Broadway musicals
______ Role in a movie
______ Complete health insurance coverage
______ Trip around the world
______ Year of study abroad
______ Acceptance to med school/law school/grad school
______ Down payment on a house
______ Happy marriage and/or family life
______ Recording contract
______ Term in government
______ A new job
______ Be a guest on *Late Night with David Letterman*

■ *Squares* by Priscilla Luming. Pass a roll of toilet paper around the group and tell each member to take as much toilet paper "as they think they need." For each square of paper they take, they must tell a joke, embarrassing moment or strange habit.
■ *Three words* by Tom Sirinides. Each person answers one or more of the following questions: If you had to describe yourself in three words, what would they be? If you had to describe your family in three words, what would they be? If you had to describe God in three words, what would they be? If you had to describe your childhood in three words, what would they be?
■ *Unique M&M game* by Amy Brooke. Everyone in the group takes one M&M for each person in their group (including themselves). They then each take a turn describing something they feel is

unique about them. (Example: "I am a twin." "I've gone rock climbing.") If someone else in the group shares that experience or characteristic, both (or more) eat one M&M. This continues until people begin to run out of candy. This activity brings to light interesting and memorable information and helps people remember each other.

■ *What's in a name?* by Tom Sirinides. Tell your full name (including middle name or Asian name) and as much as you know about it: what it means, why you were given it and so on.

■ *Zoo* by Tom Sirinides. Each person answers: What animal are you most similar to? Why?

Twenty- to Thirty-Minute Activities

■ *Brush with greatness* by Kurt Paulsen, Wis. This idea was inspired by *Late Night with David Letterman.* Each person is given a small sheet of paper. They are to write on it an experience they have had with a famous (or semifamous, or infamous!) person. This can range from simply seeing someone famous at a restaurant, or actually meeting someone famous.

After everyone is finished, scramble the papers and pass them out so that no person gets their own paper. Each person is then to "finish" the story by means of a "writer's embellishment" (they can make up whatever they want as a way to end the story).

The leader then reads each of the stories with the writer's embellishment. The group tries to guess who wrote the original story and who wrote the writer's embellishment.

The purpose of this activity is to find out something unusual about each person in a nonthreatening way. It is also a source of laughter and a good discussion starter.

This can also be used to introduce a Bible study on the Gospels or Acts. For example, if you are studying early Gospel chapters, move from this activity to looking at how people react to Jesus, a "famous person" of his day in the passage.

■ *Childhood favorites* by Irma Hider. Have each person bring something they ate while growing up. You can do this as a dinner potluck or as a snack or study break. While eating, talk about what you brought. It's great for talking about people's backgrounds.

■ *Coat of arms.* A coat of arms in the past used signs and symbols to tell something about a person or family. Make your own coat of arms, describing things about yourself. Write your answers in the appropriate spaces, or for those creative people, feel free to draw. Upper left: Two things you do well. Middle left: Your greatest success in life. Lower left: What you would do with one year left to live. Upper right: "Psychological home" or place where you feel most at home. Middle right: Three people most influential in your life or who mean the most to you. Lower right: Three words you would like said about you. Talk about your coat of arms with the group.

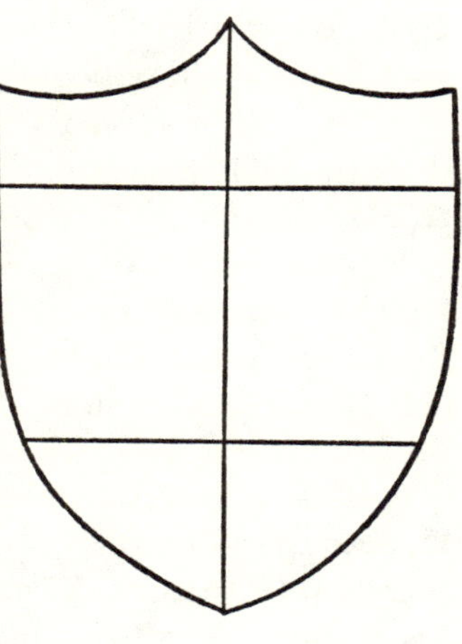

Alternate questions for each section by University of Illinois staff: What animal represents you best? If time or money were not barriers, what is the job that you would like to do most in the future? What kind of home would you like to live in? What person has had the most influence on your life? What do you like to look at the most?

■ *Collages.* Have each member make a collage, using magazine pictures and words, which describes something about themselves. If you are outside, you could gather natural materials (shells, cones, plants, sand and so on) to make the collage.

■ *Diagrams.* Think about who you are. What terms would you use to describe yourself? On a sheet of paper diagram some aspects of your personality by using small pictures. Don't worry about your artistic ability. Pair off within the group and explain your diagram to your partner. Have your partner ask you questions about your diagrams until there is a good understanding of what you are trying to communicate. Now have your partner explain his or her diagram. After the group regathers, each person should explain to the group the diagram his or her partner drew. Take time to discuss what you have learned about each other and yourself.

■ *Dinner time* by University of Illinois staff. Describe dinner at your home—where people sat, who was there, who did the talking, what the topics were. You may want to use crayons or markers to draw the table and family and use in your description.

■ *House on fire* by Tom Sirinides. Read the following scenario:

1. Your home is on fire. Everyone is safely outside and you have about one minute to run through the place to collect three or four things you would want to save. Write those things down.

2. Now tell us the items on your list and also why you chose each one.

3. What have you learned about the things that you value?

■ *Penny pass* by University of Illinois staff. Give a penny to a group member. Have all of the group members bombard him or her with his or her strengths or gifts. After a few minutes pass the penny to the next person.

■ *Roles* by Stephanie Moser. List five roles that you have in life (for example, a student, a sister, a mother). Then add an adjective that describes what kind of person you are (for example, a busy student) and another adjective describing what you want to be like (for example, a learning student). Take time to explain your adjectives.

■ *Snapshots* by Sara Keiper. An alternate way to approach the coat-of-arms exercise, especially for those who aren't familiar with or comfortable with the idea of a coat of arms, is to ask people to create a "photo album." Each photo on the page describes in words or pictures something about different parts of your life. Categories could include something about your family, three words you'd like to have said about you, where you grew up, a place you dream of visiting, three people who have influenced you the most, where you feel most at home and your favorite dessert.

■ *Tower power* by Rich Cotton, Wis. This is an active learning exercise that will provide a developing group the opportunity to cultivate relationship-building skills.

1. Divide into groups of three or four people who do not know

each other well.

2. Distribute one magazine, one newspaper section, one pencil, one ten-inch piece of string and five paper clips to each group, giving at least one item to each person.

3. Read the following directions: "You have just entered the Tower Culture, located in a very wet and often flooded area of the world. Homes in this area are in the form of a tower to keep the family up and out of the floods and away from certain reptiles or animals that may seek refuge inside. The family who uses their resources most efficiently in the form of the *tallest tower* is ascribed much honor, reverence and wisdom as *leaders of the village.*

"Each group is a family in a newly founded village. Each family member has a component needed for the building of your family tower. *You* have the power to decide how *your component* should be best used in building the tower. Your goal as a family is to build the tallest tower from the floor up, which will give you special privileges as the most respected and needed family. You have eight minutes to make decisions and complete the building of your family tower. The prestige of the family with the tallest tower will be translated into our culture in the form of not having to do the dishes all weekend." (Substitute another incentive if you are not at camp.)

4. Time them for eight minutes and tell them when two, four, six and eight minutes are up.

5. Measure the towers and declare the winning family.

6. Discussion questions:

a. Which member's participation was most helpful in the team's accomplishment of the task? Why?

b. What behaviors seemed to hinder the team's efforts?

c. What did you learn about yourself as you had to work with a very new group of people? (Discuss feelings of trust, whether they were active or passive in their participation, problems in communication, how they reacted to stress, and so on.)

d. What did you learn about other team members?

e. We will be working as a team in our learning, prayer and

emotional support. What principles and guidelines can we follow to help us develop as a team as a result of what we learned from this simulation? Write these down for all to see on an overhead or chalkboard.

Thirty-Five-Minute to One-Hour Activities

■ *Draw your hope* by Allen Lincoln. This exercise will help you evaluate your spiritual growth and see how God is working. In a small group meeting early in the year have everyone draw a tree. At the bottom, they should write in what they hope to be rooted in this semester (the world, Christian relationships, Christ's principles, prayer and so on). For the trunk, they should label how they will live that out (being part of a small group, attending church and/or fellowship meetings, working through a Christian book, regular quiet times). For the leaves, branches and flowers, they should write all the things they hope to have grown as fruit in their lives by the end of the semester (Scripture is alive to them, led someone to Christ, more at peace every day, overcome an addiction or sin). Allow people to talk about their trees with one another at a level which they feel comfortable; you might want to divide into pairs for this.

Then put the drawings away until the end of the semester. At the last meeting, pull them out again and see how your tree did! Talk about what came true, what didn't and why. What unexpected growths or fruit took place? Any sudden tree diseases hit? Offer prayers of thanksgiving for what God did during the semester.

■ *Life line.* Draw a graph which will represent your life. Thinking back as far as you can, consider the high points, the low points, moments of inspiration, moments of despair, leveling-off times and where you are now. The line will probably be a mixture of straight, slanted, jagged and curved lines. After you've drawn it, share what it means to you with others in your group.

■ *Movie making* by Sue Sage. This works if you have a couple of VCRs and a camcorder available, plus a couple of technology buffs to do the editing. This usually takes an entire evening and is at its best when it gets really late. The basic gist is to find a crazy idea and film a movie about it. Titles could include: *Star Trek: The Lost Generation, Forgiven* (a western with a happy ending) and *Without a Clue* (a mystery).

■ *Revelations: The Game for Small Groups Who Want to Go Deeper* by Cal Stevens, Ariz.

Object of game. Your group may compete against other small groups or against each other. When playing against other small groups, the object of the game is to have your team members reach 50 points as close to the same time as possible. When playing against other members of your small group, the object is to reach 50 points—without going over 50—first.

Equipment. Photocopy a Personal Inventory (see below) for each player. You also need one die and a deck of regular playing cards.

Rules.

1. Instruct each group member to rank the Personal Inventory statements from 1 to 10, giving a 1 to the statement they find easiest to complete and a 10 to the one they find most difficult.

2. Choose tokens. You may ask people to choose a token that means something special to them (a ring, a key, whatever) and share its significance with the group.

3. The oldest person begins by placing their token on *start,* rolling a die and moving the corresponding number of spaces. After they've taken the action indicated on the space where they land, play passes to the left. Keep answers to two minutes.

4. Follow instructions on playing board as follows:

Revelation: Players draw a card and answer the item on their Personal Inventory which corresponds to the number on that card. They then receive that number of points. (A two of any suit means "give your two-point answer"; a three means "give your three-point answer"; and so on. Aces serve as one-point answer cards. Ignore or pull out jacks, queens and kings.)

When someone draws a card for a question they have already answered, they must draw again. If they have answered all ten questions on their Personal Inventory, they may answer them a second time—differently, of course—for double points.

Retell Revelation: Retell the last Personal Inventory answer

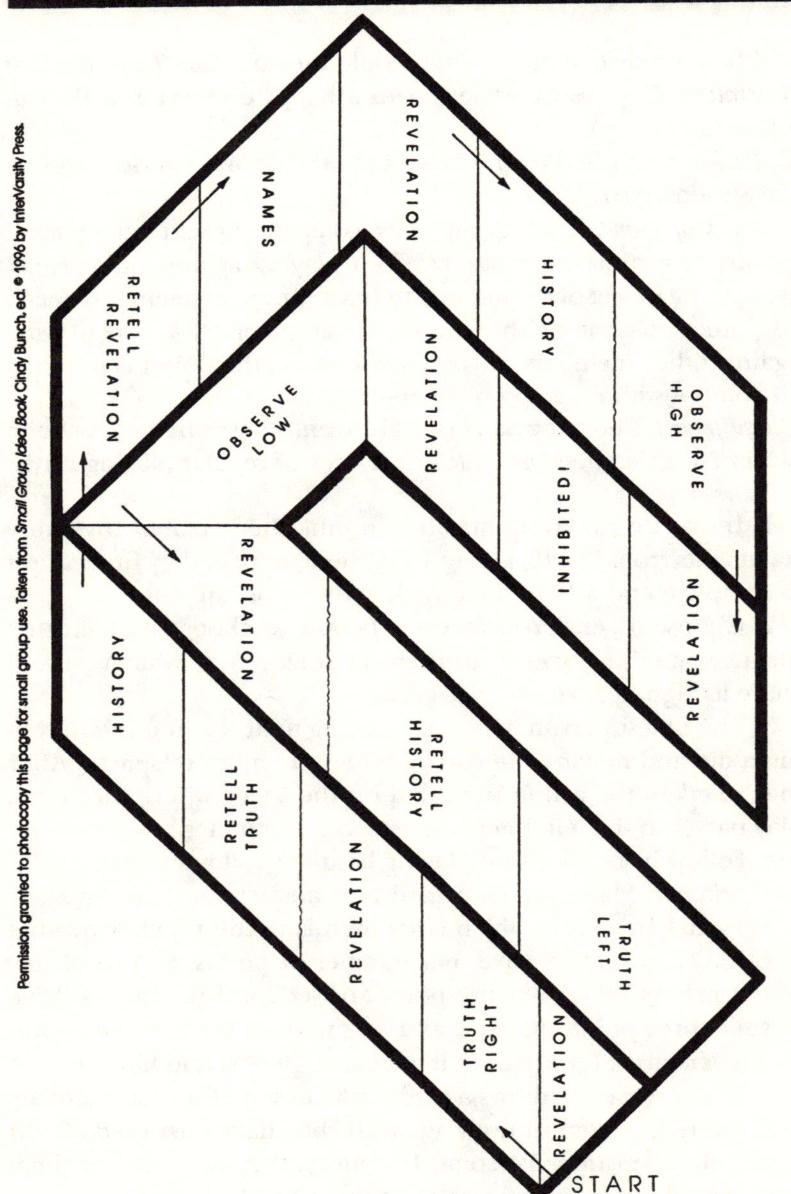
START
REVELATION
TRUTH RIGHT
REVELATION
RETELL TRUTH
HISTORY
RETELL REVELATION
NAMES
REVELATION
HISTORY
OBSERVE HIGH
REVELATION
INHIBITED!
REVELATION
OBSERVE LOW
REVELATION
RETELL HISTORY
TRUTH LEFT

given by someone else for five points.

Names: Player receives one point for each person whose first, middle and last names she can remember. Players can only get points for recalling names once; those who land on the "Names" square a second time must roll again.

Truth Right (Left): The person on the player's right or left can ask him or her anything not on the Personal Inventory. Player receives five points for answering.

Retell Truth: Repeat the last truth shared by another person for five points.

History: Give a two-minute personal history for five points. If you land on "History" a second time, tell about a completely different part of your life for ten points.

Retell History: Recap the last personal history given by another person in the group for five points.

Observe High (Low): Player observes a quality in the person who has the highest (lowest) score—even if it's himself—for five points.

Inhibited!: No points this turn.

5. When playing against other groups, one person can pass a Personal Inventory question off to a teammate to help group members' scores stay on an even par.

When playing against other members of the small group, one person can pass a Personal Inventory question off to someone else to keep from going over 50 points—as long as that question does not push the other person's score over 50 points.

In either case, the person who receives the question gets the same number of points that the original player would have received. If the person to whom the question is passed has answered it before, they must answer it again, differently, for double points. Each player can pass off questions no more than three times.

6. If playing on teams, group members determine how many points away from 50 they are when someone on their team ends their group's playing time by scoring 50 or more points; this value is totaled and divided by the number of players to figure the average deviation. The group with the lowest average deviation from

50 wins. (Other small groups do not have to be present for you to compete against them. In fact, you may want to set up a small-group "tournament" in which each group plays the game during a particular week early in the semester, then reports their average deviation score at the next large-group meeting.)

7. When playing against other members of your small group, the game ends when someone hits exactly 50 points and wins, or goes over 50 points and loses. If no one scores exactly 50 points, the person with the score closest to 50 wins.

Personal Inventory
Complete the following statements, and then rate them according to how difficult they are to complete. Give the one you find easiest to complete a 1, the most difficult a 10.
Ranking
_____ The dumbest thing I ever did was ____________________.
_____ The best thing about me is ____________________.
_____ One thing I'll do differently from my parents is __________
____________________.
_____ One thing I'd like to change about myself is __________
____________________.
_____ This depresses me: ____________________.
_____ I wish I could ____________________.
_____ Family is ____________________.
_____ My friends consider me ____________________.
_____ I experienced love when ____________________.
_____ My favorite music artist/group is __________ because
____________________.

■ *Trust walk* adapted by Tom Sirinides. Divide the group into pairs. (You could use prayer partners or people who don't know each other well.) Blindfold one person in each pair. Each unblindfolded person leads a blindfolded person around the general vicinity of your meeting place. Try to provide many different experiences—take them up some stairs, go outside and inside, help them feel different objects, walk at different paces, walk on different materials (grass, floors, dirt), but say nothing after the walk has started. You must nonverbally communicate all messages. For example, when you get to some steps, stop before the step and lift the person's arm slightly to indicate a rise.

After about five minutes, change places and blindfold the other person. After another five minutes regather the group. Discuss what kinds of feelings you had as you were blindfolded and as you touched objects. Here are some questions you can use (if you use all of them you will need twenty to thirty minutes):

☐ How did it feel to lead?
Did you sense a lack of trust?
How did you seek to build trust?
What was difficult about leading?
What made it hard to lead?
Did you develop any signals?

☐ How did it feel to be led?
Did you trust the other person?
What helped you to grow in trusting them?
Did you try to keep track of where you were all the time while blindfolded?
Did you peek?
What was it like to have no control over what was happening?
Did the other person ever let go or leave you? If so, what did you do?

☐ Who preferred leading? Who preferred being led? Why?

☐ What did you learn about yourself in all this? about how you relate to and trust God? about how you relate to and trust other people?

■ *Twenty loves.* Give each person a piece of paper. Allow a few minutes for all group members to list twenty activities they enjoy doing. Some may find they have far more than twenty; others may have trouble listing five. Encourage them to think about what they enjoy doing most. For some that may even be daydreaming.

After they have made their lists, have each make the following notations next to each item to which it applies:

A—things which you prefer to do alone

P—things you prefer to do with other people; if others are involved, put names of others with whom you most enjoy this activity

$—those which cost money to do (over $1)

R—items which have some element of risk involved (physical or personal)

S—activities which are sedentary (more quiet or passive)

M—those which are active

C—things which take some form of communication to do

L—items you had to learn to do—a skill you had to acquire

CH—activities you did as a child

PA—activities that at least one of your parents does or did

Look at your list and rank the activities. As you look over your results, what do you notice about yourself? What repeated aspects come out, particularly in your top five? Is there anything you hadn't realized before?

Here are more specific questions you could ask:

1. Do you most enjoy doing things by yourself, with others, or both?

If with others, are there people you continually enjoy being with? friends? family? members of the same sex? members of the opposite sex? Are there people you consistently enjoy doing a variety of things with? Do you usually enjoy one-to-one time, small groups or large groups?

2. Do the things you enjoy usually cost money?

3. Are you a risk taker? What kind?

4. Are you sedentary, active or a mixture?

5. Do you do many things that require communication? Are you often with people doing things that don't require communication?

6. Are there skills you have had to work at to do things you enjoy? Are those items in your top five or lower on your scale? Do you most enjoy things which you can do naturally?

7. Are you enjoying things you learned as a child and that your parents did? What things have changed since childhood? What have you built on?

8. Looking at your list, which of these would be hardest for you

to give up? Which would you miss the most if you didn't do it?

Now take about ten minutes to discuss your findings with one other person in the group. If those in the group know each other fairly well, you could stay together.

Note: There are no good or bad answers in this exercise. The purpose is simply to see ourselves and to share what we see with others.

When the group pulls back together, share with the whole group what you saw about yourself, particularly if you saw something you hadn't realized or thought about before. Have each person say at least one thing he or she particularly enjoyed learning in talking with his or her partner.

■ *Warm up.* Explain to the group that the following questions will help us get to know one another better. They are not loaded but simply represent a way to get to know each other in a short time. Take one set of questions at a time. The leader can begin by answering first and then go around the circle with each answering each set of questions.

Set 1:

1. What is your name? (If you did this earlier, do it again so names can be learned quickly.)

2. Where did you live between the ages of seven and twelve years?

3. What stands out most in your mind about the school you attended at that time?

Set 2:

1. How many brothers and sisters were in your family between the ages of seven and twelve years?

2. During your childhood, how did you like to get warm when you were chilled or cold? Perhaps after an afternoon of skating, skiing or sliding? Or early mornings at a cabin or out camping?

Set 3:

During your childhood, where did you feel the center of human warmth was? Was it a room or a person? (For example, the TV room when your family was all together? the kitchen?) It may not have been a room at all; it may have been a person around whom you sensed safeness and warmth.

(The leader may want to mention that some people do not remember a center of human warmth in the home. This may put at ease people for whom this was true. Was there another center of warmth for them?)

Set 4:

(This question is asked to the group as a whole and you do not need to go in a round for this. Let people answer as they feel comfortable; some may choose not to answer at this time.) When, if ever, in your life did God become more than a word? When did he become a living being, someone who was alive in your own thinking?

(This may not be an account of a conversion. This transition in one's thinking can happen before actual conversion or after. It may have happened in conversation with a person who loved them, or in a worship service or listening to music. This is not a time of discovering the whole counsel of God, but simply a time of personal awareness.)

As you conclude this discussion, point out in summary how our different experiences bring us to different points in our growth and in our experiences now.

Although our security and acceptance begins with physical warmth and graduates to human warmth, we are never complete until we find security in God.

If time is short and this is not your first meeting, omit Set 1 and the first question in Set 2.

■ *"Who am I?"* Make a list of eight items which identify who you are or significant aspects and roles of your life. (Examples: student, son, friend, helper, writer, critic, etc.)

Then consider each item in your list. Try to imagine how it would be if that item were no longer true for you. (For example, if you were no longer a son or daughter—loss of both parents—what would that mean to you? How would you feel? What would you do? What would your life be like?) After reviewing each item in this way, rank the items by writing a number to the right of each item. Order them according to the importance this role has to you at this time. Which would most drastically effect your life if it were taken away? (1 is most important, 8 is least.)

Finally, share your results with one person in your group. Tell each other how you came to your decisions. Be as open as you can. Then regather as a group. Discuss the following: Is there something about yourself this exercise has taught you? As you thought over the questions of loss of an item, did you realize some things you hadn't before? What role was most significant for you? Why? Then let the person you talked with tell the group one thing he or she appreciated about you from what you said.

Ideas for shake-up

These ideas are specifically designed to help the group process conflict and deepen their trust.

■ *Blessing* by Stephanie Moser. After the group has known each other quite awhile (maybe a semester), focus on one person at a time, and have everyone share adjectives or words that describe how you have seen God in their life. It is a time of affirming who they are and the qualities God has given them. After five to ten minutes on that person, offer prayers of thanksgiving for him or her.

■ *Inside/Outside* by Tom Sirinides. Have the following ready: a lunch bag for each person, newspapers and magazines, tape or glue, and scissors. Let people cut out words and pictures about themselves. On the outside of the bag put things that describe the way you think others see you; on the inside put things that describe the way you see yourself.

■ *Sociogram.* Each person in your group relates to each other person in a unique way. There are some in your group who are very close; there are others who hardly know each other. It will help you in ministering to your group if you know where there is strength in relationships and where there are needs. Making a sociogram is one way to find out. Some observations will be evident; others may not be. More than likely, group members' feelings about these dynamics will not be known.

You can approach making a sociogram in two ways: (1) You can do it alone or with a coleader, small group coordinator or staff worker. In this way you can pinpoint some needs and look for ways to help build relationships. In the same light you can see how the group has helped build relationships. Doing a sociogram at least two to three times a year will help you see growth. (2) You can work through a sociogram with your group. Having the whole group involved in this process can give additional (and often more accurate) information. It also can lead to discussing why some problems and feelings exist. As a group, you can then be committed to building a more solid community.

To make a sociogram:

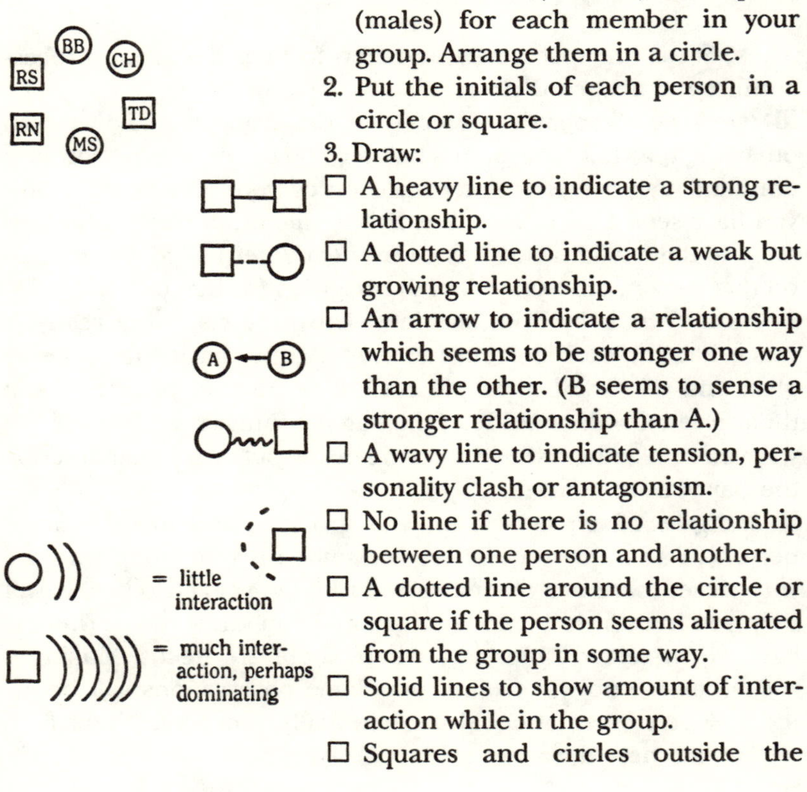

1. Make a circle (females) and square (males) for each member in your group. Arrange them in a circle.
2. Put the initials of each person in a circle or square.
3. Draw:

☐ A heavy line to indicate a strong relationship.

☐ A dotted line to indicate a weak but growing relationship.

☐ An arrow to indicate a relationship which seems to be stronger one way than the other. (B seems to sense a stronger relationship than A.)

☐ A wavy line to indicate tension, personality clash or antagonism.

☐ No line if there is no relationship between one person and another.

☐ A dotted line around the circle or square if the person seems alienated from the group in some way.

☐ Solid lines to show amount of interaction while in the group.

☐ Squares and circles outside the

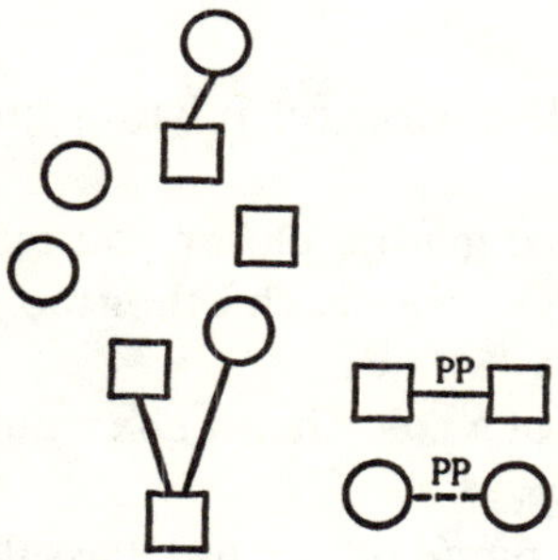

PP
PP

group which indicate close relationships which may or may not take members away from the group.

4. Mark prayer partnerships.

5. Also note the following characteristics:

☐ Personality (introvert-extrovert and so on).
☐ Who takes the most/least initiative in discussions?
☐ Who takes initiative in unstructured times?
☐ Who is open about him or herself?
☐ Identify real needs of the group.
☐ Identify potential growth in the group.

6. What do you do with this information?

If you make a sociogram by yourself or with one other person:

☐ List the obvious (people who are not closely relating to anyone in the group or tensions in the group).
☐ Look at your resources for dealing with these needs. Is there a relationship forming? Is there tension and is one of these people an initiator? Could they take initiative in beginning to work through some problems? Does the group need some more fun times together? Who is your social organizer?
☐ Begin to talk with some of these people about the needs you see and how they could be of help in this.
☐ Pray for love, wisdom and guidance as you pray through each relationship and take steps to grow.

If you make a sociogram as a group, ask:

☐ What new things have you seen about yourself or the group as a result of this exercise?
☐ How did this make you feel?
☐ What do you see as the needs of the group?
☐ What resources do we have as a group to meet these needs?
☐ What should we do to strengthen our community life?

Ideas for live-it-up

These exercises will help you with self-disclosure, relating and celebrating one another's gifts.

■ *Color me.* As your group members are getting closer you may need to encourage them to share feelings about each other more. This exercise can help.

1. Take time for each person to think of a color he or she would use to describe each person in the group.
2. Take a piece of paper and put your name on the top. Pass the paper randomly so each person can put the color he or she associates with you on it. Then return the sheet to the person whose name is on the top.
3. Let one person at a time respond to the colors they've been given. Give the rest a chance to explain why they gave a certain color, particularly if it differs from what others have given.
4. Each can ask for clarification as needed.

If you want to be more direct, you could ask what feeling you have when you think of each individual person in your group. Then go around and give this feedback. If there are feelings which need to be worked on—hurt, distance, hostility—talk about it and confront any problems. (If your group is ready for this, it could create a much closer community and move you to the live-it-up phase.)

■ *Dinner together* by Sue Sage. As a closure celebration, you might prepare a fancy dinner for the group. Some more creative twists have been to dine in a church fellowship hall, to have someone act as chauffeur and come to pick up all the members and transport them to the dinner, and to use the time for the members to affirm each other.

■ *Discovering spiritual gifts.* "And his gifts were . . . to equip the saints for the work of the ministry, for building up the body of Christ" (Ephesians 4:11-12 RSV). Take time to help people identify gifts God has given and how each can be used in your fellowship by using this worksheet. Encourage each other by providing opportunities to use gifts in your group.

Worksheet for Discovering Spiritual Gifts

Read Romans 12:6-8. Then respond to the questions below.

Things I like to do for others:

1. ______________________________

2. ______________________________

3. ______________________________

4. ______________________________

5. ______________________________

Things I do which God seems to bless:

1. ______________________________

2. ______________________________

3. ______________________________

People I would like to be like:

1. ______________ 3. ______________

2. ______________ 4. ______________

What abilities (gifts) do these people have which I admire?

1. ______________ 3. ______________

2. ______________ 4. ______________

What do other people affirm about apparent gifts God has given me? (Ideally, your small group will take time to share with each member the gifts they have observed and tell what they have appreciated about their use in the small group. If it is not possible to do this in a group, an individual can try to recall what others have appreciated.)

1. ______________________________

2. ______________________________

3. ______________________________

4. ______________________________

5. ______________________________

Plan to practice (for their improvement) the gifts you seem to have.

What?	When?	Where?
1. ________	________	________
2. ________	________	________
3. ________	________	________
4. ________	________	________
5. ________	________	________

■ *Encouragers* by Priscilla Luming. Do a secret encouragement project for the leaders in your church or fellowship by sending small gifts, Bible verses and thank-yous from others.

■ *Group journal* by Paul Thigpen (adapted from *The Small Group Letter,* issue 3, vol. 10). Encourage group members to make a journal entry in a notebook each week after they get home from the meeting or allow time for this during each meeting. Make it voluntary so that it doesn't become burdensome. You may want to decide at the beginning how long you will keep the journals.

The entries need not be long, but they should record whatever was important to the writer about what took place: insights gained, decisions made, humorous anecdotes, particular feelings about what was said or done—anything goes. Members can read their entries aloud to the group on occasion; shared observations are meaningful to a group.

■ *How I receive encouragement* adapted from *How Do I Say I Love You?* by Ann Beyerlein. This is a short exercise to help you determine what type of encouragement is most meaningful to you. Rank the types from 1 to 8, 1 being the most important to you. Then discuss this in your small group.

Ranking	Area of Encouragement
	Meeting material needs
	Helping
	Spending time together
	Meeting emotional needs
	Saying it with words
	Saying it with touch
	Being on the same side
	Bringing out the best

Complete each sentence.

1. When down and in need of support, I like someone to . . .
2. It hurts my feelings most when someone does not . . .
3. I feel a sense of acceptance and worth when someone . . .

■ *Question in the hat* by Ann Beyerlein. Each member writes down a question and puts it in a hat. The hat is passed around and each member takes out a question and answers it.

■ *Sentence completion* by Nina Thiel, Nev. Choose enough sentences for everyone in the group, write them down, fold them up and put them in a hat. Send the hat around and have everyone pick one, then have everyone complete their sentences.

I feel comfortable with people who . . .
I know I can trust someone when . . .
I feel cared about when . . .
I feel lonely when . . .
A friend is someone who . . .
When I am sad, it helps if someone . . .
The people I'm closest to . . .
It's hard for me to open up to people when . . .
In a group I like to . . .
At times I am afraid to reach out to others because . . .
If I could improve my relationship with others, I would . . .

■ *Valentine's Day* by Nina Thiel. Draw a heart on a half sheet of paper and divide it into five sections. (Two or three hearts can fit on one sheet.) Photocopy them on pink or red paper and cut them out and give one to each member. Complete each of the sentences below, writing your responses in the sections. After giving some time to answer the questions, each person can share his or her heart.

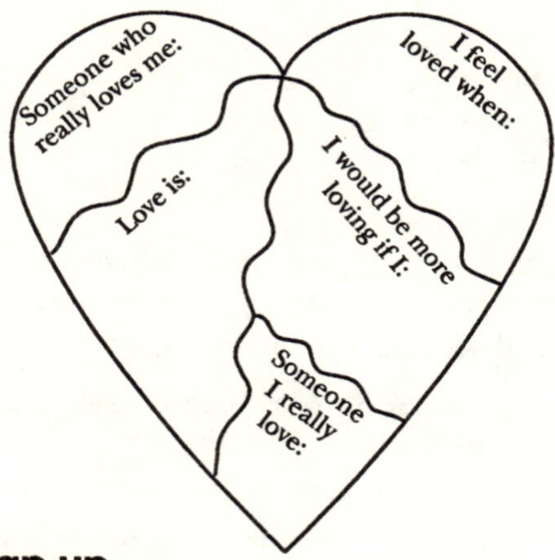

Ideas for wrap-up

These ideas are designed to help the group affirm one another's gifts, experience closure and celebrate what God has done in the group.

■ *Appreciation demonstration* by Sara Keiper, Penn. Each person takes enough blank sheets of paper for everyone in the group. On one side draw a picture, Bible verse, prayer, word, phrase, sentence, or whatever will show the person what you have appreciated about them. On the other side of the paper draw a picture, Bible verse, prayer, words, or whatever will demonstrate what you wish or hope for them.

■ *Foot washing* by Sue Sage. This is a simple yet powerful way of expressing care for someone. Take a basin and towel, go around the circle and have each person wash the feet of the person next to them. This goes well with a small group worship time or when studying the crucifixion.

■ *Gift giving* by Sara Keiper. A week or so in advance, talk about giving gifts to show appreciation of each other and what you have experienced together. Giving a gift does not necessarily mean buying one. The best ones are usually made. A gift could be a special Bible verse made into a bookmark, a certificate to do laundry for a specified period of time, or a picture from a magazine that is symbolic—the possibilities are limitless. Encourage people *not* to buy things, or at the very least set a cost limit. (For some, choosing to buy can be significant.)

Have one person sit in the center of your small group circle. Each person then gives to this person an intangible gift or Bible verse which reflects something they would like to see them have, an area in which they would like to see them grow, or a reminder of a special time or quality. Give the gift and explain why you are giving that gift. Each member of the group takes turns being in the center. Close in a time of thanksgiving and prayer for one another. You may want to lay hands on each person as you pray for them.

■ *Gift making* by Nina Thiel. A week before the group's last time together for the semester, have everyone draw names and spend the week making a gift, such as a bookmark, card, hand-painted T-shirt, poster or keepsake box. You might also pick out one special verse from the book of the Bible you have been studying or based on a character from Scripture and offer a blessing: "May you be like ___________, who . . ." For example, see Ruth 4:11-12.

■ *Group history* by Paul Thigpen (adapted from *The Small Group Letter,* issue 3, vol. 10). A great idea for groups that have been together for a long time or are ending, this project offers a sense of closure and puts things into perspective. Either at home or in a meeting each member writes a summary of his or her experience in the group as if it were a chapter in a history book. Focus on fond memories, critical junctures and the overall patterns of the group's experience. What was the happiest moment in the group? What challenges were overcome? What directions or central concerns took shape as the group developed? What are the most important lessons they learned? What contribution has the group made to their relationship with God? Allow people to keep their writing private if they want to.

■ *Growth.* Have each member discuss one area where they have been growing during the past three or so months together. Then have them look ahead into the next three months. Ask, "In what one area would you like to see yourself grow most (or continue growing most)?" Pray for each person concerning their area of growth.

■ *Memorial stones* by Sara Keiper. Bring enough rocks (not gigantic ones) for everyone in the group. Have each person pick one. Read Joshua 4, or tell the story and read just a few verses in summary. Then have each person tell ways they have seen God's faithfulness, and place their rock on the growing pile. Conclude your time thanking God for his faithfulness.

Variation: Bring markers and have people write a word or draw something symbolizing God's faithfulness. After making the memorial and praying let people take their rocks home as a visual reminder of God's faithfulness.

■ *People celebrations* by Sue Sage. This activity involves a small group spending some time celebrating a certain person's life. Celebrations could include the whole group's eating that person's favorite meal while listening to the music of their choice and coaxing out of them some childhood stories. You could follow this with doing that person's favorite activity. Try including handmade gifts for that person and a time of prayer for them.

■ *Praying Scripture* by Sara Keiper. Using prayers and other Scriptures, pray specifically for each person in your group. Prepare for this by asking God to lead you to particular passages for each person. Another way to do this is to let the group pick out prayers for each other, or let each person choose what they want the group to pray for them.

Here are just a few suggested passages: Numbers 6:24-34; Deuteronomy 33:26-29; Psalms 20 and 67; Isaiah 43:1-5; Lamentations 3:22-23; Romans 8:38-39; Ephesians 1:17-19; 3:14-19; 5:15-20; Philippians 1:6; 1:9-11; 3:12-14; 4:4-6; 4:8-10; Colossians 1:9-12; 1 Timothy 6:11-12; 1 Peter 5:6-7. You may also want to choose a passage from the book you've been studying in the group.

■ *Strength bombardment.* This exercise is designed to let you express the positive feelings you have for each other by pointing out the strengths you see in others. This is best done after you have gotten to know each other fairly well.

First, ask one person to remain silent while the others concentrate on this person and bombard him or her with all of the things that you like or see as a strength. Keep bombarding the first person with positive feelings until you run out of words.

Then, move on to the next person in your group and do the same until you have covered everyone in your group.

After everyone has finished, ask, "How did you feel when you were the focus of bombardment? Don't evaluate what was said about you, but tell how you felt about getting the feedback." Then ask, "How did you feel about giving feedback to others?"

■ *Thank-you notes* by Sara Keiper. Give each person attractive pieces of stationery, so that each one has enough sheets for a note to the others in the group. Have people write words of appreciation, a Bible verse or whatever else they are thankful for. Have each person be "it." Each one in the group reads their note to that person, followed by a group prayer thanking God for him or her.

■ *A ticket for your thoughts* by Nina Thiel. Everyone in the small group gets a ticket (you can photocopy the one at the right), and no one can be asked a question twice until everyone has been asked a question once. Questions can range from light to heavy, and the answerer has the right to ask for a different question if they feel uncomfortable with the one they are first asked.

> This **TICKET**
> Entitles the bearer to the answer to one question of his/her choice when given to another member of his/her small group.

■ *Yearbook page* by Nina Thiel. Ask someone to take a picture of the whole small group well before your last time together for the semester or year. Develop and make enough copies for everyone. Glue the photographs on nice pieces of cardstock. Include the names of everyone in your small group, the year, and so on. At your last time together, bring out the cards plus lots of pens and give everyone a chance to write on each other's pages.

Books on Community

Bonhoeffer, Dietrich. *Life Together.* Translated by John Doberstein. New York: Harper & Row, 1984. Classic account of the experience of Christian community in an underground seminary during the Nazi years. Discusses the role of prayer, worship, work and service in community.

Griffin, Em. *Getting Together.* Downers Grove, Ill.: InterVarsity Press, 1982. A guide for groups of all sorts to discover what makes a group good. Covers conflict, deviance, persuasion, expectations, leadership and how to have a good discussion.

Icenogle, Gareth. *Biblical Foundations for Small Group Ministry.* Downers Grove, Ill.: InterVarsity Press, 1994. In-depth biblical survey of Christian community and how it works in small groups.

Lofink, Gerhard. *Jesus & Community.* Philadelphia: Fortress Press, 1984. Jesus' model of forming community with the disciples.

Peck, M. Scott. *A Different Drum: Community Making & Peace.* New York: Touchstone Books, 1988. The author describes his journey toward finding community with several different groups.

Serendipity (Box 1012, Littleton, CO 80160) publishes books and a Bible for groups with ideas for community-building experiences. Write for an order form. Some ideas in Serendipity are from Bible studies and can give ideas of combining application and community from our passage.

Snyder, Howard. *The Community of the King.* Downers Grove, Ill.: InterVarsity Press, 1977. Explores the relationship between the kingdom of God and the church in our daily lives.

Suggs, Rob. *Christian Community.* A LifeGuide® Bible Study. Downers Grove, Ill.: InterVarsity Press, 1994. Twelve studies on what Christ's body, the church, is designed to be and how we find our gifts and experience worship, healing and God's power.

Swihart, Judson, J. *How Do You Say, "I Love You"?* Downers Grove, Ill.: InterVarsity Press, 1977. Describes eight different languages of love. Especially for married couples, but others can benefit.

2
WORSHIP & PRAYER RESOURCES

Taken from *Preacher from the Black Lagoon* by Rob Suggs (Downers Grove, Ill.: InterVarsity Press, 1991) and used by permission.

■ *Attributes of God* by Carol Johnson. Go around the group, having each person take the next letter in the alphabet to describe an attribute of God. Read Psalm 145.
■ *Bible reflection.* Look back at the passage you have studied and ask what things it has shown about God or what attributes of God we see in this passage. Praise him for these aspects of his character.
■ *The Book of Common Prayer.* This historical resource of the church is full of material which can be used to guide a group into worship and prayer. Following are samples of what's there.

A General Thanksgiving
Accept, O Lord, our thanks and praise for all that you have done for us. We thank you for the splendor of the whole creation, for the beauty of this world, for the wonder of life, and for the mystery of love.

We thank you for the blessing of family and friends, and for the loving care which surrounds us on every side.

We thank you for setting us at tasks which demand our best efforts, and for leading us to accomplishments which satisfy and delight us.

We thank you also for those disappointments and failures that lead us to acknowledge our dependence on you alone.

Above all, we thank you for your Son Jesus Christ; for the truth of his Word and the example of his life; for his steadfast obedience, by which he overcame temptation; for his dying, through which he overcame death; and for his rising to life again, in which we are raised to the life of your kingdom.

Grant us the gift of your spirit, that we may know him and make him known; and through him, at all times and in all places, may give thanks to you in all things. *Amen.*

Corporate Confession (contemporary form)
Most merciful God,
we confess that we have sinned against you
in thought, word, and deed,
by what we have done,

and by what we have left undone.
We have not loved you with our whole heart;
we have not loved our neighbors as ourselves.
We are truly sorry and we humbly repent.
For the sake of your Son Jesus Christ,
have mercy on us and forgive us;
that we may delight in your will,
and walk in your ways,
to the glory of your Name. Amen.

■ *Break with tradition.* Doing things differently can enhance your time of worship. Perhaps plan to meet at a neighborhood church one evening and use the sanctuary or chapel as a place of worship. Kneel as you pray. Lift your hands to God. Take a nature walk and pray as you walk together, thanking God for what you see. Use creative dance or drama as a form of worship. Be original.

■ *Concerts of prayer.* Commit to spending several hours on a Saturday morning or a weekend evening or even a whole day or night in prayer for the world. InterVarsity students may want to commit to spending time in prayer for the work of IFES (International Fellowship of Evangelical Students) around the world. Church members may want to pray for the missions program of their denomination. Or group members may want to pray for friends who are missionaries. Prayers might also focus on national and international revival. Here are a few steps to putting it together (adapted from IFES materials by John Rogers and a *Student Leadership* article [Winter 1993] by Marie Paretti and Jeff Yourison).

1. Mark the date. World Student Day is February 24. The National Day of Prayer is the first Thursday in May. Various denominations have designated days of prayer for their ministries.

2. Choose the planners. Your group may want to plan the event for a larger group of people or for yourselves. Be sure to plan prayerfully and with good communication. Get input from the prayer warriors in your group and any ministry teams which might play a role.

3. Use existing structures. Make the concert of prayer part of a

regular meeting or time of worship.

4. Get information on the group you are praying for. Invite missionaries and/or Christian international students to come and speak. Check out resources from your denomination. *Operation World* by Patrick Johnstone has significant facts about missionary movements in every part of the world as well as information on planning concerts of prayer. Consider how to provide this information during the course of your time of prayer to help participants know how to pray.

5. Plan creatively. Use ideas that fit your context. Here are a few that have worked in the past:

- ☐ Reserve a comfortable place on campus or in your church to pray throughout the day, and have people sign up for shifts during the day so that a continual prayer goes up to God.
- ☐ Organize an extended meeting time for a large or small group including times of worship and praise, singing, silent and vocal prayer. Break into smaller groups at times, then return to the larger group.
- ☐ Invite churches in your area to join in or have their own concerts of prayer on the same day.
- ☐ Develop a short talk or skit to describe the ministry you are praying for and how your group fits into the bigger picture. The ten-minute IFES video *Students Reaching Students* is a great resource for campus.
- ☐ Bring in needs and concerns you notice in newspapers and magazines. Pray for specific local needs as well as global needs.
- ☐ Find out what a day in the life of a person from a country you are praying for would be like. You might have a meal together to sample the food from a particular country.
- ☐ Have a world map on hand, and mark it to show unreached countries and specific places you're praying for.
- ☐ Take an offering to support a missionary in another country.

6. Plan effective follow-up. Encourage people to keep praying, perhaps by organizing a monthly or weekly prayer meeting. Get involved in a partnering relationship with a church or IFES chapter in another country. See the section on revival prayer. You may

want to commit to this discipline individually and/or as a group.

■ *Create a psalm* by Kelle Ashton, Ill. Begin by reading a few psalms that are meaningful to you. Then have everyone write the first verse of any psalm on the top of a piece of paper. Each person passes their paper to the right. The next person reads the verse and adds one to it from their own thoughts, trying to build on the previous verse. Continue passing the papers around until everyone has added to each psalm. Read each psalm.

Jane Bacon of California suggests another psalm-writing method based on Psalm 107: After reading Psalm 107, look at the four categories of people described there (vv. 4-9, 10-16, 17-22, 23-32). Note the format of each of these groups of verses:

Some ________________ (description of people).
They were ________________ (description of sinful actions).
Then they cried out to the Lord and he delivered them from __________. Let them give thanks for ____________ (God's work).

Challenge each person to write their own stanza of this psalm *or* several stanzas describing periods of their life. Then read them to the group. End in praise for how God continues to know us, hear our cries and deliver us.

■ *Devotional readings.* J. I. Packer's *Knowing God,* A. W. Tozer's *The Knowledge of the Holy* and J. B. Phillip's *Your God Is Too Small* are excellent choices. Read short excerpts which will direct your thoughts to God and give time for the group to respond in worship. These prayers can open or close times of prayer. Richard Foster has put together spiritual readings which show how great men and women of the faith have responded to the character of God in *Devotional Classics.*

Here's an excerpt from *Knowing God* (pp. 41-42):

What matters supremely is not the fact that I know God, but the larger fact which underlies it—the fact that *he knows me.* I am graven on the palms of his hands. I am never out of his mind. All my knowledge of him depends on his sustained initiative in knowing me. I know him, because he first knew me, and continues to know me. He knows me as a friend, one who loves me; and there is no moment when his eye is off me, or his attention distracted from me, and no moment, therefore, when his care falters.

This is momentous knowledge. There is unspeakable comfort—the sort of comfort that energizes, be it said, not enervates—in knowing that God is constantly taking knowledge of me in love, and watching over me for my good. There is tremendous relief in knowing that his love to me is utterly realistic, based at every point on prior knowledge of the worst about me, so that no discovery now can disillusion him about me, in the way I am so often disillusioned about myself, and quench his determination to bless me. There is, certainly, great cause for humility in the thought that he sees all the twisted things about me that my fellow humans do not see (and am I glad!), and that he sees more corruption in me than that which I see in myself (which, in all conscience, is enough). There is, however, equally great incentive to worship and love God in the thought that, for some unfathomable reason, he wants me as his friend, and desires to be my friend, and has given his Son to die for me in order to realize this purpose.

■ *Examining your conscience* by St. Ignatius of Loyola. In *The Spiritual Exercises of St. Ignatius* we find a five-point method for "the daily examination of conscience" in prayer. This can be used in your group, and you can challenge one another to keep this discipline personally.

1. I thank you ____________________.
2. I need you ____________________.
3. I love you ____________________.
4. I am sorry ____________________.
5. Stay with me, Lord!

■ *Fasting* by Northwestern University students. The Bible defines fasting as a Christian's voluntary abstinence from food for spiritual purposes. Jesus makes it clear that he expects us to fast. In Matthew 6:16 he begins by saying, "When you fast." Also, this teaching about fasting in the Sermon on the Mount directly follows his teaching on giving and praying. It is as if it were assumed that giving, praying and fasting are all part of the Christian devotion.

We cannot use fasting to impress God (or others) or to earn his acceptance. We are made acceptable to God through Jesus' work, not ours. Fasting pointedly reveals the things that control us, whether that be our stomachs, pride, anger, bitterness, jealousy, selfishness, fear—the list goes on. Fasting reminds us that, instead, we are sustained "by every word that comes from the mouth of God" (Matthew 4:4). Food does not sustain us; God sustains us. When the disciples, assuming that he was hungry, brought lunch to Jesus, he said, "I have food to eat that you know nothing about. . . . My food . . . is to do the will of him who sent me and to finish his work" (John 4:32, 34).

Richard Foster writes in *Celebration of Discipline:*

> Therefore, in experiences of fasting we are not so much abstaining from food as we are feasting on the word of God. Fasting is feasting! . . . We are told not to act miserable when fasting because, in point of fact, we are not miserable. We are feeding on God, and just like the Israelites who were sustained in the wilderness by the miraculous manna from heaven, so we are sustained by the word of God.

Fasting does not change God's hearing so much as it changes our praying. There's something about it that sharpens and gives passion to our intercessions. Fasting also makes us more receptive to God's guidance and wisdom. The church in Antioch "fasted and prayed" before they laid their hands on Barnabas and Saul and sent them off on the first missionary journey (Acts 13:3).

There are also many other purposes of fasting, such as expressing grief, seeking deliverance or protection, expressing repentance and a return to God, humbling oneself before God, overcoming temptation, expressing love and worship to God, and so on. In all of this, God will reward those who diligently pursue him.

A small group could decide to do a prayer fast together beginning after lunch on a given day. During the dinner hour, the following Bible study could be used.

☐ Read through Psalm 145 and jot down all the characteristics of

God you see in the passage.

☐ Take some time to praise God for the characteristics in the passage.

☐ Then read Acts 4. Below are some prayer requests based on that passage.

—Personal: that knowledge of Scripture would grow for God's glory (vv. 8-11), that we would have the boldness of Peter and John to speak to friends and neighbors about Christ (vv. 19-20)

—Christian community: that prayer would be the first thing on our minds (v. 24), that the Holy Spirit would shake us to speak the Word of God boldly (v. 31), that we would exemplify the community of believers to our community (vv. 32-35)

—Community: that people in our neighborhoods and on our campuses would recognize their sinfulness (v. 10), that people would acknowledge that Jesus is salvation (v. 12), that Jesus would reside in our community (vv. 29-30)

That evening a small group could meet to process the day, discuss what God has taught them and pray together again.

■ *God hunt.* Spend a few minutes reflecting on the past week, looking for times that God has worked in your life, answered a prayer or been present in a way you overlooked at the time. Listen to each person's experience, then pray in praise for these things.

■ *Guided reflection* adapted from Doug Stewart by Northwestern University students. Something like this could be used in a small group retreat time.

After the group comes back together after a time of personal reflection:

☐ Read and ponder Psalm 107 as an example of remembering, reflecting and learning from God's interventions in our history.

☐ Draw in a lifeline of the flows and movements of your spiritual life over the past three or six months. Fill in significant events and activities. Express the high as well as the low periods. What characterized the high periods? What characterized the low periods? Remember what was happening in and around you at those times. Do you see any constants or patterns?

What have been recurring or major struggles in your life this past year? Any painful failures?

What growth or progress have you seen take place?

☐ Remember that growth in grace often seems to be like going backwards as we discover new areas of need and experience new grace. This is often as we go through hard, often embarrassing and painful experiences. In the midst of this, we find grace to cover us and to carry us through. Often too, the awareness of growth is known only to us and is not so visible to others. Growth can take the form of seeing recurring areas of defeat lessen their hold on us. Growth can be seen as old fears are faced and set aside, or as old wounds are acknowledged and healing begins. Old patterns (often from childhood) are acknowledged and renounced, and new patterns are initiated.

Some constants of true growth in grace are:

(1) deepening trust in God as we face life's threats, choices and uncertainties.

(2) deepening awareness and experience of the love of God toward us, resulting in more freedom and inner wholeness.

(3) deepening, more resilient hope in God's promises and power in the face of the forces of evil which confront us, reresulting in more patience and steadfastness.

☐ Try to summarize a couple of the basic things which God has been showing you or teaching you during this time.

What significant decisions or turning points have you come to?

☐ Remember to write down specific blessings received, for which you can give thanks and praise to God. Be ready to share one of these blessings with the small group this day.

■ *Healing prayer* by Roy Lawrence, U.K. (taken from *The Practice of Christian Healing*). The laying on of hands has always had a central place in the ministry of Christian healing. It is natural to touch those we are seeking to help or comfort. Scripture tells us that Jesus incorporated this natural ingredient of human care into the heart of his healing ministry. For instance, after the healing of Peter's mother-in-law, "When the sun was setting, the people brought to Jesus all who had various kinds of sickness, and laying his hands on each one, he healed them" (Luke 4:40). Jesus expected his followers to incorporate the laying on of hands into the heart of their healing ministry (Mark 16:18).

When you pray for someone, put one or both hands on that person's head and pray something like: "Father, let these hands of mine convey the touch of Jesus, the love of Jesus, the healing power of Jesus—*(name)*, I claim all that God has in his generous heart for you here and now. God our Father and Creator recreate you by his mighty power in body, mind and spirit. God the Son, our Lord Jesus Christ, meet you at your point of need and hold you in his strong and loving presence. And the healing influence of God the Holy Spirit, Lord and Giver of life move within you, freeing you from all that could hurt you and bringing you new life at every level of your being. The blessing of God Almighty, Father, Son and Holy Spirit, rest upon you, surge within you and bring you wholeness, joy and peace. Amen."

My expectation is that when there has been prayer with the laying on of hands, there will always be blessing and strengthening unless the Lord is resisted. Often the blessing and strengthening will be accompanied by some sort of physical, mental or spiritual healing. This may be either total or partial.

■ *Hymns and songs.* Instruct or remind people to think of themselves as speaking to God as they sing. Read a song rather than sing it for a change of pace. Use familiar songs at your first few meetings. Keep a list of those your group knows. Give background material if it is helpful. Have members concentrate on one or two main themes which run through the hymn. Point these out ahead of time so the group's attention is drawn into focus. Study the hymn to see what Scripture is referred to. For example, at Advent "O Come, O Come, Emmanuel" would be appropriate. At Easter "When I Survey the Wondrous Cross" or "O Sacred Head" would be especially meaningful. Hymns like "And Can It Be," "Jesu, Lover of My Soul," "Amazing Grace" and "O for a Thousand Tongues to Sing" call us to worship and wonder at what God has done for us. And "Guide Me, O Thou Great Jehovah" and "Be Thou My Vision" call us to commitment as we seek God's will.

■ *Intercessory prayer* by Paul Hughes, Fla. A significant aspect of your small group will be praying for one another's needs. An intercessor is one who stands in the gap between God and the world and bears the burden to pray. Studying the following outline and passages will give you courage to exercise spiritual authority through prevailing prayer.

☐ Entering God's Throne Room

1. Enter confidently in Jesus' name (1 Timothy 2:5; Hebrews 4:14-16; 5:7-10)
2. Enter continually (Luke 11:9-13; Philippians 4:6; Colossians 4:2; 2 Thessalonians 1:11)
3. Enter privately (Matthew 6:5-6)
4. Enter with a pure heart with no unforgiveness (Matthew 6:14-15; 2 Corinthians 2:10-11), no selfish motives (James 4:3; Philippians 2:3-4) and no unconfessed sin (James 5:16)
5. Enter with others (Matthew 18:19; Acts 2:42)
6. Enter with the Word of God (Daniel 9:1-3; Ephesians 6:17-18)

☐ How to Intercede

1. Pray to the Father in Jesus' name (John 14:8-14; Acts 4:5-12)
2. Pray with the help of the Holy Spirit (Romans 8:26-27; Ephesians 6:17)
3. Pray on the offensive with God's agenda in mind (Matthew 16:18; Ephesians 6:18)
4. Know the enemy's power (Romans 8:37-39) and weapons (John 8:44; Revelation 12:10), and pray against the powers and principalities (Ephesians 6:12-13)
5. Know the Lord (Luke 10:18)
6. Have confidence in the blood of the Lamb (Revelation 12:11)
7. Pray with worship and praise (2 Chronicles 20:18-22)
8. Pray in unity with other believers (John 17:20-23)
9. Combine prayer with fasting (Acts 13:2; 14:23)

■ *Journaling.* Completing a journaling exercise as a group and discussing it can be very rewarding. It can be an important step in introducing members to a new discipline that can be used personally as well. Here are some possible journaling topics.

☐ How have you been aware of God's presence in your life today? this week? this month? this year? throughout your life?

- ☐ What have you learned about God recently?
- ☐ What are your future goals—one year, five years, ten years?
- ☐ What would you say if you could ask God any question? Why?
- ☐ Describe the most significant person in your family. Is your relationship with that person positive or negative? How has it impacted you?

Richard Peace has created a journaling guide especially for group use called *Spiritual Journaling.* It includes group discussion questions, journaling exercises and group Bible studies. It's a great tool for introducing a group to this spiritual discipline.

■ *The Lord's Prayer* by Patty Pell, Colo. Use each line of the Lord's Prayer as a guide for a few minutes of group prayer. For example, after "hallowed be thy name" is read, worship by using various names for God in praise. Work through the entire prayer in this way.

■ *Meditation.* Use the "approach" exercises in Spiritual Encounter Guides by Stephen D. and Jacalyn Eyre (IVP) to help the group focus their thoughts and quietly prepare for study. Discuss your experiences before you begin the rest of the group time. Here are a few samples from *Entering God's Presence.*

- ☐ Make a list of things that are on your mind that come between you and God right now. Lift each one up to the Lord and ask him to take them.
- ☐ Joyce Huggett writes of being in God's presence and hearing God call her name. "Sometimes it seemed as though Jesus himself stood in front of me or beside me or above me. . . . The only way I can describe it is to liken it to [what] a person feels when they love someone very deeply. . . . No words are necessary. They might even be intrusive, for they could trivialize the love."

  Sit quietly for a few moments. If you can enter into the silence described above, write down a few words to describe it. If you can't enter silence yet, write down the distractions that you feel and give them to the Lord.
- ☐ Imagine that you are in a desert and in need of water. You see a well in the distance and head for it. How do you feel? Now

see your heart as the desert and the Lord as the well. Write down your responses.

You can also use meditation to close your group or end a Bible study. Stephen Eyre titles these sections "Reflect." Here are some samples from *Waiting on the Lord.*

☐ David writes that he has "become like broken pottery" (Psalm 31:12). At one time or another we have all felt shattered and broken by the events of life. Perhaps you still feel that way (although the events happened a long time ago). Imagine that you are a broken pot. Sit quietly for a while and allow God to put your life back together. After a time of reflection, write down your observations.

■ *Mood-breaking prayer.* Have you ever arrived at small group to discover a gang of grouches awaiting you? In *Daily Guideposts 1994* Ellen Secrest suggests "mood-breaker prayers" for those times. The key to these prayers is to focus on lifting up the needs of others. Soon you'll find that your mind is more in tune with God's.

■ *Names of God* by Lisa Overby, S.D. Bring 5 × 7 index cards, paper and pencils or pens for everyone and pass them out. Ask everyone to write down all the names of God they can think of. (This can also be done with the attributes of God.) Give a time limit of three to five minutes. When everyone is done, ask those who are comfortable to list the names they have written down. As you go around, everyone can add each others' names to their lists. Each member will have a "names of God" postcard when they're done. It'll look something like this:

> All-Mighty, Forgiving, Creator, Provider, Most High God, Friend, Eternal, Conqueror, Faithful, Seeker of My Heart, Always There, Peacemaker, A Prayer Away

Talk about why these names are significant to members of the group. Make this a basis for your prayer and praise.

This is very encouraging for the seeker, believer and especially the small group leader. Save the cards and do the activity again later in the year to discover how you are learning about God.

Below are listed some names of God from *Knowing God by His Names: A 31-Day Experiment* by Dick Purnell (Here's Life Publishers) to give you a sample of the riches that can be found in Scripture. Another way to use these names in worship is to encourage the group to quietly reflect on one verse or one name of God.

Names	Characteristics	Key Passage
Adam, the Last	Different from Adam and his descendants	1 Corinthians 15:45-47
Advocate	Helper, divine lawyer who pleads our case	1 John 2:1-2
Almighty	All powerful	Revelation 1:8
Alpha and Omega	Beginning and end of everything good	Revelation 22:13
Amen	God's final seal of His promises	Revelation 3:14
Ancient of Days	Judge of the whole world	Daniel 7:9
Angel of Jehovah	Old Testament appearance of Christ	Genesis 16:7-11
Anointed	Messiah	Psalm 2:2
Apostle	The divine representative	Hebrews 3:1
Author and Perfector of Faith	Origin of salvation, leader, developer	Hebrews 12:2
Beginning of the Creation of God	Origin and source of the universe	Revelation 3:14
Beloved	Perfectly and uniquely loved by God the Father	Matthew 12:18
Beloved Son	God's own unique one	Matthew 3:17
Blessed and Only Potentate	Honored sovereign	1 Timothy 6:15
Branch	Divine origin, descendant of David	Zechariah 6:12
Bread	Satisfies our hunger for life and eternity	John 6:35
Breath of the Almighty	Spirit gives life and strength	Job 33:4
Bridegroom	Betrothed to the Church, His bride	Mark 2:19, 20
Bright Morning Star	Brilliant, awesome	Revelation 22:16
Chief Shepherd	Foremost of all leaders	1 Peter 5:4

■ *Personal pet peeves* by Irma Hider. The leader bakes green sugar cookies and makes green paper circles. Have each person write down their pet peeve about themselves—short-tempered, talks too much, envious. These are *character* issues. Then tell each other what you have written. Exchange papers with your prayer partner or someone else in the group. The other person will commit to praying for the person's pet peeve. Pray as a group that God would help you, and then eat the green cookies. A few weeks later have people share how it is going *if* they want to. Do this to edify, *not* to put down those who have been struggling.

■ *Prayer partners* by Cindy Meyers. God has promised that when two or three of us gather in his name, he will be there with us (Matthew 18:19-20). How can we draw near to God? How do we spur one another on toward love and good deeds? Through praying together (1 Thessalonians 5:17-18) and bearing one another's burdens (Galatians 6:1-2).

Prayer partners are not just "bowling buddies" who meet regularly to participate in an activity. A prayer partnership is not a new form of Christian dating. While engaged and married couples certainly should pray together, men and women who are not already committed to each other should probably not form a prayer partnership. A prayer partnership is not a substitute for one's personal relationship with the Lord. Prayer partners sometimes help to balance one another, but they never stand on one another's shoulders. Their sole foundation is always the Lord Jesus himself.

Prayer partners *are* Christians who have committed themselves to an open and honest relationship. It is in some ways risky but it is a risk that the Lord honors when two people become serious about meeting with him and growing together. As with any serious relationship, to build a prayer partnership costs time.

The priority of this relationship also affects their willingness for the partnership to grow. Few prayer partners begin as David and Jonathan. Few prayer partnerships begin with complete honesty and perfect trust. But expect growth—and growing pains.

Prayer partners:

☐ Describe specifically what the Lord has taught them and what they know the Lord is trying to teach them.

- ☐ Talk purposefully, avoiding a mere social session of aimless gabbing.
- ☐ Pray specifically for one another's needs, for plans and for common concerns.
- ☐ Pray purposefully, expecting God to act in their lives and willing to be used of God in answering their prayers.
- ☐ Pray habitually, looking to the Lord as a first response to situations rather than as a last resort.
- ☐ Pray for each other through the week and not just when together.

■ *The prayer tree* by Hallie Cowan, Mass. The prayer tree is made of paper or wood (be creative) which is hung on a wall or put in a stand so that paper leaves can be attached to it. Each leaf contains one prayer request and the date it was written. Each request must be specific, so you can tell when God has answered the prayer. (Not "God bless my roommate," but "Find a ride home for Jim.")

Keep no more than two or three current requests per group member on leaves at one time. The group can agree together when and how to add leaves for concerns they all want to pray for. If you meet daily, you may want to keep the leaves in a central "leaf box." If you meet weekly, you could hand out leaves so one person can pray daily for each request. When a prayer is answered, add the leaf to the tree as a sign of God's provision and your thanksgiving. (If the answer is no, you can hand the leaf off to the side or under the tree.)

Groups report that when the first leaf goes up on the tree, there is real excitement and a desire to pray more. Then, as more and more leaves are added, the enthusiasm continues to grow! With a prayer tree you can "see" that God really does answer prayer!

■ *Prayer chains.* When someone in your group has an urgent need or concern between meetings, it's great to be able to get in touch with others in the group. Establish a prayer chain in your group with a key contact person. Once that person is contacted, he or she will get in touch with the next person on the list and so on. Each person needs to remember only who he or she is to call. Contacting a key person in each small group can also be a great way to get prayer concerns out to the whole church or fellowship.

■ *Prayer walks* by Patty Pell. Divide into groups of two and three and walk around the campus or the community near a group member's home. As you walk, pray conversationally for the people who live and work in the buildings you pass, bless the houses and dorm rooms, pray for people you see. Listen for the prompting of the Holy Spirit to show you how to pray.

■ *Praying a psalm* by Allen Lincoln. One person reads a verse, then silence is allowed where people can respond vocally or quietly. People might pray a rephrase of the verse or a reminder of something else to pray for—it can be very stream-of-consciousness. After enough time has passed, the next person prays the next verse. This can be an opening to a small group meeting or be the whole meeting itself.

■ *Read the headlines* by Lisa Boegner, Mich. Cut out several headlines from various sections of a recent newspaper. Distribute the headlines to the group members. Then, have each member come up with a spiritual application to the headline. For example, a headline that reads "A Sure Victory, a Not So Sure Thing" could be associated with how everyone thought Goliath surely was going to beat David, but "a sure victory is not so sure a thing," especially when God is in control. It can also be used to remind us that when we try to do things on our own, without God, God may transform what we see as a sure victory into a learning experience.

■ *Responsive readings.* Hearing the Scripture read and giving a verbal response can be very powerful and can bring new insight. Many psalms are structured as liturgies of praise. For example, Psalm 136:1-6:

> Give thanks to the LORD, for he is good.
> *His love endures forever.*
> Give thanks to the God of gods.
> *His love endures forever.*
> Give thanks to the Lord of lords:
> *His love endures forever.*

to him who alone does great wonders,
His love endures forever.
who by his understanding made the heavens,
His love endures forever.
who spread out the earth upon the waters,
His love endures forever.

The psalm continues in this format for twenty-six verses. At the end you could add: "Give thanks to the Lord, for ________" (something you are focusing on in your group) with the response "His love endures forever." Other psalms can be used in this way simply by having the leader and the group alternate reading verses.

Responsive readings can also be found in hymnals and other worship resources. The "Litany of Worship" that follows is by Laura Urban, a member of a small group that was studying Joshua. You may want to create similar readings to celebrate and summarize what are you are learning as a group. This litany can be read responsively and individuals can fill in something personal in the blanks at the end:

It was the Lord our God himself who brought the Israelites out of Egypt.
Far be it from us to forsake the Lord to serve other gods!
It was the Lord our God himself who drive out other nations to give our spiritual forefathers the Promised Land.
Far be it from us to forsake the Lord to serve other gods!
It was the Lord our God himself who gave us a land in which we did not toil and cities we did not build, and we live in them and eat from vineyards and groves that we did not plant.
Far be it from us to forsake the Lord to serve other gods!
It was the Lord our God himself who forgave our rebellion and our sins and brought us from darkness into light.
Far be it from us to forsake the Lord to serve other gods!
It was the Lord our God himself who established his throne in heaven, and his kingdom rules over all.
Far be it from us to forsake the Lord to serve other gods!
It is the Lord our God himself who wraps himself in light as with a garment; he stretches out the heavens like a tent.

Far be it from us to forsake the Lord to serve other gods!
It was the Lord our God himself who set his love with those who fear him.
Far be it from us to forsake the Lord to serve other gods!
It was the Lord our God himself who sent Jesus to be the priest to offer for all time one sacrifice for sins and who sits at the right hand of God.
Far be it from us to forsake the Lord to serve other gods!
It was the Lord our God himself who ______________________
____
____.
Far be it from us to forsake the Lord to serve other gods!
WE TOO WILL SERVE THE LORD, BECAUSE HE IS OUR GOD.

(Based on Joshua 24; Psalm 103—104; Hebrews 9—10.)

■ *Revival prayer* by Dave Bryant. (Taken from "An Amazing Prayer Movement Signals Hope for World Revival" in *World Evangelization,* September/October 1994, p. 9.) This is a fifteen-minute daily discipline of revival prayer.

- ☐ Rejoice (one minute)—praise God for what he has done, is doing and is getting ready to do in world revival.
- ☐ Review (five minutes)—read books, magazines, other literature and most of all the Scriptures to learn all you can about the nature of revival, its impact on missions and its current manifestation around the world.
- ☐ Repent (one minute)—confess to God on your behalf, and on behalf of the whole church, the specific ways in which we are hindering world revival.
- ☐ Resist (one minute)—target prayer to those points where Satan is attempting to undermine the life and mission of the church.
- ☐ Request (five minutes)—drawing from the vast reservoir of biblical promises, intercede for full revival in the church—both your own and in other nations.
- ☐ Recommit (one minute)—reflect on all that you have learned from the Lord and all that you have said to him, and commit yourself back to him to be used in answer to your prayers.

☐ Record (one minute)—keep a journal to record whatever you sense God has said to you. What new understandings of revival has he given you? What new directions has he given for prayer? How has he encouraged you to influence others?

■ *Silent reflection* by Mary Hays, Penn. The leader introduces each time of silent reflection with phrases like: Reflect on the past twenty-four hours and pray silently. Thank God for what he has done in these hours. Praise God for what you have seen of God's character in these hours. Confess things you've done to separate yourself from God. Pray for the person on your right . . . on your left.

■ *Take out the garbage* by Lisa Boegner. For this you need several sheets of paper and a garbage bag. Hand out the pieces of paper and have everyone write some sin in their life that they want to get rid of. Then have someone pray. Next, have each person wad up the piece of paper and throw it in the garbage bag. This is to symbolize getting rid of the trash in our lives.

■ *Tapes and CDs.* Select favorite songs of praise from contemporary Christian artists. You can learn songs together this way or simply play them to set the tone for the beginning of a meeting. You might also play classical pieces by Bach or Handel for silent reflection or find recordings of favorite hymns.

■ *Temperature reading* by Bob Wolnicak, Wis. (From "Why Pray Together," *Student Leadership,* Fall 1993, p. 17.) To gauge how you are doing with prayer as a group, discuss how people are feeling about prayer. What do they know about it? How does it affect them? Ask if anyone has a prayer experience they'd like to talk about. Ask what part members would like prayer to play in the group. Then study a passage about prayer such as Matthew 6:5-15; Mark 1:35-39; Luke 11:1-13; John 17 or Nehemiah 1. Your discussion and study will show you where you are weak and where you are strong in your prayer life together.

■ *Victory prayer* by Charles Stanley, Ga. In his book *The Wonderful Spirit-Filled Life* Stanley encourages us to claim God's promise of victory before we face predictable battles as well as in the midst of them. This prayer can encourage group members who are struggling with temptation and complement studies dealing with spiritual battles.

> Lord, I claim victory right now over the giant of ________. I recognize that this giant is coming against the Christ in me. Just as You defeated this giant when You walked on this earth, you can defeat it through me now, for You are my life. I trust You to produce peace and self-control through me. When the pressure comes, remind me that the battle is Yours. Amen.

■ *Wish prayer* by Elsie Larsen, Ore. (Taken from *Daily Guideposts 1994,* p. 201.) In Isaiah 65:24 we read, "Before they call I will answer; while they are still speaking I will hear." God knows our wishes—what we hope for—before we even realize we should pray for them. Since I discovered what can happen when I wish something good for someone, wishing has become fun for me. Every greeting card I send is really a wish and a prayer. Throughout the day, as I see a need, I offer wishes for others like good thoughts blown their way. The rest I leave to God. He understands and answers.

Your group could offer "wish prayers" for one another as a way of showing understanding and offering encouragement. It will be exciting to see what God does as you dream of the Lord's best for one another.

■ *Worship poster* by Nina Thiel. Get a large poster board or five-foot piece of butcher paper. Bring colored markers, magazines, scissors and glue. Have everyone gather around and make a visual representation of praise to God, each on their own "corner" of the poster. They can make a collage, draw a picture, write a verse and so on. Put it up on the wall when everyone's done.

■ *Writing.* Sometimes it is helpful to collect our thoughts and write them down. Think over the last day or two. List things for which you are thankful. Share your list with the group. Have members lead in prayer as they praise God with what they have written. Write letters of gratitude to God; share parts of them; pray them conversationally back to God.

Creative writing can also be a help in worship. Give group members time to write a poem, song or psalm. Read them to each other, using them as an introduction to worship.

Books and Music for Worship and Prayer

Alexander, Donald L. *Christian Spirituality*. Downers Grove, Ill.: InterVarsity Press, 1988.

Beckwith, Paul, Hughes Huffman and Mark Hunt, eds. *Hymns II*. Downers Grove, Ill.: InterVarsity Press, 1976. A collection of hymns—some old, some new. *Hymns II* is packed full of praise and honor to God. Guitar chords are given.

Bounds, E. M. *Power Through Prayer*. Chicago: Moody, 1985 (reprint).

Companion Songbook for Prayer and Worship for Small Groups. Wholehearted Worship, P.O. Box 850242, Mobile, Ala. 36685 (205) 660-7288.

Eyre, Stephen and Jacalyn. Spiritual Encounter Guides, Downers Grove, Ill.: InterVarsity Press. These quiet time guides focus on worship and prayer. You may want to use some of the exercises in your group.

Foster, Richard. *Celebration of Discipline*. San Francisco: Harper & Row, 1978. Insightful writing on twelve key spiritual disciplines.

______. *Prayer: Finding the Heart's True Home*. San Francisco: Harper & Row, 1992. Looks at what prayer is and how it works in our lives.

Foster, Richard, and James Bryan Smith. *Devotional Classics*. San Francisco: Harper & Row, 1990. Readings from writers like Bernard of Clairvaux, St. Augustine and C. S. Lewis with Bible passages and discussion questions.

Gregg, Doug, and Mike Flynn. *Inner Healing*. Downers Grove, Ill.: InterVarsity Press, 1993. Focuses on healing prayer.

Hallesby, O. *Prayer*. Minneapolis, Minn.: Augsburg, 1959. Discusses our motivation for prayer and what God wants to teach us about himself through prayer.

Huggett, Joyce. *The Joy of Listening to God*. Downers Grove, Ill.: InterVarsity Press, 1986.

Integrity Music, Inc. P.O. Box 5205, Clifton, N.J. 07015-9785. Instrumental and vocal tapes, CDs and printed music for worship.

Johnstone, Patrick. *Operation World*, fifth edition. Grand Rapids, Mich.: Zondervan, 1993. A daily guide to praying for the world with facts about missions in every part of the world.

Marshall, Catherine. "Prayer of Relinquishment." *Guideposts,* March 1993, reprinted from October 1960. Deals with the question of unanswered prayer and giving up our will for God's will.

McNeill, Morrison, and Henri Nouwen. *Compassion.* New York: Doubleday, 1992.

Packer, J. I. *Knowing God.* Downers Grove, Ill.: InterVarsity Press, 1973. Packer asks: What were we made for? What aim should we set in life? What is the best thing in life? What in us gives God the most pleasure? And the answer to all these questions is to know God. As Packer teaches us about God we are led to worship. Focus on the section "Behold Your God."

Packer, J. I. *Meeting God.* A LifeGuide® Bible Study. Downers Grove, Ill.: InterVarsity Press, 1986. Twelve inductive Bible studies focusing on the character of God.

Patterson, Ben. *Worship.* A Christian Basics Bible Study. Downers Grove, Ill.: InterVarsity Press, 1994. Six inductive studies on the biblical basis of worship.

Peace, Richard. *Spiritual Journaling.* Colorado Springs, Colo.: NavPress, 1995. A resource for groups who want to learn to journal together. With individual exercises, group discussion questions and Bible studies.

Peterson, Eugene. *Answering God: The Psalms as Tools for Prayer.* San Francisco: Harper & Row, 1989.

Piper, John. *The Pleasures of God.* Portland, Ore.: Multnomah, 1991. In chapter eight, "The Pleasure of God in the Prayers of the Upright," Piper emphasizes that it is not we who meet God's needs in prayer, but God who meets our needs: "The way to *please* God is to come to him to get and not to give. . . . He is most glorified in us when we are most satisfied in him" (p. 216).

Postema, Don. *Space for God.* Grand Rapids, Mich.: CRC Publications, 1983.

Rinker, Rosalind. *Learning Conversational Prayer.* Liturgical Press, 1992.

Ryan, Dale and Juanita. *Recovering from Distorted Images of God.* Life Recovery Guides. Downers Grove, Ill.: InterVarsity Press, 1990.

An inductive Bible study that leads people to consider how their view of God has been distorted by family and church experiences and to have their vision transformed by Scripture.

Tozer, A. W. *The Knowledge of the Holy.* New York: Harper & Row, 1978. "Written for plain persons whose hearts stir them up to seek after God Himself." Each chapter begins with a prayer and ends with a verse. The chapters are designed to help us appreciate God, especially his majesty and holiness.

Trevethan, Thomas L. *The Beauty of God's Holiness.* Downers Grove, Ill.: InterVarsity Press, 1995. In a book that is at once a manifesto and a devotional guide, the author vividly reminds us that holiness is an essential characteristic of the biblical Lord. He carefully describes the true shape of God's majesty, then devotes several chapters to life before the Holy One—living as if God really is the center of all creation.

Wallace, Daniel B. "Who's Afraid of the Holy Spirit?" *Christianity Today,* September 12, 1994, pp. 35-38. A skeptical Dallas Theological Seminary professor explores the charismatic movement and discovers anew how God works in the world today.

Webber, Robert. *Worship Is a Verb.* Nashville: Star Song, 1992. Defines worship as an active expression of the Christian faith as a community.

Webber, Robert. *Worship Old & New.* Grand Rapids, Mich.: Zondervan, 1994. Shows how the traditions of the early church can be applied in meaningful ways to worship today.

White, John. *Daring to Draw Near.* Downers Grove, Ill.: InterVarsity Press, 1977. White examines ten prayers from the Bible and helps us learn about prayer, God and those praying.

3
NURTURE RESOURCES

"Next time, let's make sure the ice-breaker doesn't include questions about politics."

■ *Acting* by Kelle Ashton, Ill. When studying a Gospel or Acts, have each person take a different part instead of reading the passage. Act out the passage together as a group and discuss how each person felt and the insights they gained from acting instead of reading.

■ *Applying the Word* by Bill Clark, Calif. To be sure you don't miss the important step of application, study a Scripture passage one week and then focus on applying the passage the following week. For example, after studying the lifestyle of the early church in Acts 2, one small group was convicted by the level of care the new believers had for each other's practical needs. The group brought a box to IVCF large group meeting and encouraged the fellowship that if anyone had a need to make it known. Requests were placed in the box and the small group mobilized the chapter to help meet those needs.

■ *Bible charades* by Irma Hider. Put names of books of the Bible in a hat for a game of charades. Or use this as a summary of the book or topic the group has been studying. You might want to ask the group members to write down the topics to be acted out.

■ *Bible study*. Bible study will probably be the main source of nurture for your group. But don't let your creativity stop here. Vary the kind of study you do over a period of time. Include an inductive study of passages on similar topics, a character study, a manuscript study (see order information on p. 80), a study of a book of the Bible, a study using a guide (see listing on p. 81). You may want to intermix some of the other ideas in this section (booklet study, videos) for a different focus for a week or two.

■ *Booklet study*. Many of the small booklets by InterVarsity Press are excellent for group discussion. Two, *My Heart—Christ's Home* and *Tyranny of the Urgent*, have companion Bible study guides: *Commitment* and *Priorities*. Write for a catalog: IVP, P.O. Box 1400, Downers Grove, IL 60515.

■ *Collages* by Sue Sage. This is a creative way to express almost any idea that you have been focusing on—a Scripture passage, an element of your community life, answers to prayer. All you need are scissors, glue, magazines and paper. Have each person explain their collage, and you will learn a lot about him or her!

■ *Conferences.* Attend a conference oriented to small groups and Bible study through Bible & Life (for IVCF, see the description on page 77), the annual small group conference cosponsored by Fuller Seminary and Eastern College (locations rotate) or Pilgrimage/NavPress Small Group Training developed by Richard Peace (one-day seminars sponsored across the U.S.—call 1-800-477-7787). Prayerfully support each other throughout the event and hold one another accountable for personal commitments made at the conference. Afterward, talk about it over pizza.

■ *Contrasts* by Margaret Parker, Calif. (Adapted from "Exploring Contrasts" in *Student Leadership,* Spring 1990, p. 11.) God inspired the biblical writers to present vivid contrasts—light versus darkness, life versus death, love verses alienation—to highlight the crucial choices before us and help us choose rightly. You can help group members experience the persuasive, life-changing power of God's Word by focusing their attention on the contrasts in Scripture. For example, with the parable of the prodigal son (Luke 15:11-32), ask people to list every contrast they can find in the passage. Then have them choose one area of contrast and explore it more fully. Be sure people understand that they can use their imaginations to flesh out the various elements of the contrast.

Suppose your group explores the differences between the life the prodigal son led in the far country and the life he found waiting at home. As they imagine what the prodigal must have experienced, they will find the parable draws a sharp contrast between two kinds of partying. The phrases "squandered his wealth in wild living" (v. 13) and "no one gave him anything" (v. 16) suggest that in the far country the prodigal tried desperately to buy fun and friends, but instead found only fleeting, dehumanizing pleasures followed by painful disillusionment and abandonment. How different from the homecoming party that greeted his return, where real pleasures (hugs and kisses, new clothes, a great feast, music and dancing) were given freely to the prodigal as expressions of his father's love for him, a love that nothing he had done could ever cancel out. These contrasts can lead to the personal application that our choice is not between partying and God, but between joyful, lasting fellowship and illusory fun.

■ *Emotional impact* by Margaret Parker, Calif. (Adapted from "Recapturing the Bible's Emotional Impact" in *Student Leadership,* Winter 1988, p. 13.) The Bible is personal communication, God speaking to us through the voices of people in history. As a leader, you can help group members be sensitive to the emotional content of the passages they study. One way to foster this sensitivity is to suggest that they listen for tones of voice and visualize facial expressions as they read God's Word. Or have a group member read dramatically as they feel its author would have spoken it. Have the rest of the group imagine they are members of the original audience hearing the message for the first time and talk about how they would have responded. This approach works well with the poetry in the Bible, particularly Psalms and the Prophets (see, for example, Isaiah 1:2, 13, 18). The Epistles also often convey emotions (see Galatians 4:9-11). Strong emotional currents also underlie the historical narratives in Scripture (see Luke 7:36-50).

■ *Experience.* Each of us has ways in which God has been working in us and different experiences in dealing with doubt, pain, death, joy, love and so on. Share these with each other so others can benefit and grow from one another's experience. Remember one person's experience is not descriptive of what every other person's experience will be or should be. God meets us as individuals. This time is to help us encourage one another, not prescribe cures.

■ *Intergenerational study.* Some groups find that they enjoy including family members in part or all of their meetings. Doing Bible study with children can be tricky, but IVP has developed a series called LifeGuide® Family Bible Studies which is designed for adults to do with grade-school children. Each study includes an introduction, the passage in the International Children's Version, seven inductive questions, a pencil/paper activity, a prayer suggestion and a bonus activity. The eight guides are *The Friendship Factory; Fruit-Filled; God's Great Invention; Good Choice, Bad Choice; Grown Up on the Inside; Jesus Loves Me; Super Bible Heroes* and *The Wisdom Workshop.* For adults and teenagers we have a Family-Based Youth Ministry Curriculum, *Bridges,* which is designed for an hour or more in group discussion and interaction.

■ *Jesus' family* by Irma Hider. This is a great way to begin studying Matthew or any of the Gospels. Don't tell the group that this is about the genealogy of Jesus. Give individuals or pairs different Scriptures to look up dealing with one of the following key characters. (How many you use depends on how many people are in the group.) They are responsible for reporting back to the group in three to four minutes what they learned about their character. The characters are:

Rahab	Joshua 2:1-24; 6:20-25; Hebrews 11:31; James 2:25
Jesse	1 Samuel 16:1-13
Naomi, Ruth, Boaz	Ruth 1:1-22; 2:11-12; 4:13-22
Judah, Tamar, Perez	Genesis 38:1-19
Moab	Genesis 19:30-38
David	2 Samuel 11:1-27; 12:15-18
Abraham	Genesis 12:1, 11-13; 16:3-15; 21:1-3
Isaac, Jacob	Genesis 25:19-26; Hebrews 11:8-10

As people tell what they learned (in no particular order) try to find some ties between the family, personal and spiritual histories of the characters. By the end you will have read about incest, murder, adultery, a prostitute and the promises of God. After you are done with this, read the genealogy of Jesus (Matthew 1:1-17). By this time some members of the group will have started to catch on. The point is to see that Jesus' family is made up of broken, sinful people, and we are each descendants of Christ. In the same way he accepted his ancestors and the roots from which he came, he also accepts each of us as members of his family no matter what sinfulness may be a part of our past. Reflect on Romans 8:14-17 and Galatians 3:29 and offer prayers of thanksgiving that we are children of God and heirs with Christ.

■ *Scripture memory.* Use one of the following: Learn a psalm a month. Memorize one verse or passage from the book you are studying. Use Topical Memory System (NavPress, P.O. Box 20, Colorado Springs, CO 80901).

■ *Stepping into Scripture* by Nairy Ohanian. This activity expands our knowledge of biblical characters and godly attributes, as well as our understanding of one another. Ask the group who their favorite biblical heroes and heroines are. Have them either draw this character as they imagine them to be or simply write the name of the person on paper. Next to each drawing or name, have everyone write what they respect about the person. Have each person talk about how they relate to this person and in what ways they want to be like the person. Have the members in the group pray for each other, specifically asking God to fill them with the desired qualities of their Bible hero or heroine.

■ *Tangent ball.* This idea is for a group whose members are pretty comfortable with each other, probably in the live-it-up phase. At the beginning of the study give one member a Nerf ball (or a wad of paper). During the Bible discussion, if another member goes off on a tangent, the holder of the ball throws it at that person. That person is then in charge of the ball. This is a good way to give control of the study to the group members and takes the burden of keeping the study on track off the leader. The tangent ball should *not* be used when someone is talking about his or her life, a deep concern or a prayer request.

■ *Tapes.* Listen to a tape and have four or five questions ready for discussion. You can order tapes on a wide range of topics from TwentyOneHundred. Write P.O. Box 7895, Madison, WI 53707 for an order form.

■ *Training.* Train your group to do inductive Bible study using *Discovering the Bible for Yourself* by Jeffrey Arnold. Use *Leading Bible Discussions* and *Small Group Leaders' Handbook* (all IVP) with one or two potential leaders in the group. Rotate leadership among those you are training.

■ *Quiet times.* Encourage one another to do quiet times by using the Daily Discovery system (see p. 78). You may also want to work through the quiet times in Stephen Eyre's *Drawing Close to God* and follow his suggestions for discussing your quiet time experiences in a group. Or use the daily quiet times in *The NIV Quiet Time Bible* to prepare for the book you are studying in your small group.

■ *Videos.* TwentyOneHundred Productions produces a variety of videos for college students and church members with user's guides that include summaries and suggestions for discussion. For example, "Give Me an Answer" with Cliff Knechtle, "Speaking of Jesus" with Mac Stiles and "Voices of a Generation" (about Generation X) give help in the area of evangelism. "Ripped Down the Middle" deals with dysfunctional families, and "Out in the Open" is about sexuality. "Beyond Church Walls" and "God Is Building a City" encourage us to reach our communities. "Face to Face" addresses the need for racial reconciliation. Write to InterVarsity Video, P.O. Box 7895, Madison, WI 53707-7895 or call 1-800-828-2100 or visit the IVCF Web site at http://www.gospelcom.net/iv.

Tools for nurture

■ *Bible & Life.* Bible & Life is an intentionally focused series of training weekends and on-campus follow-up to help equip students by the power of the Holy Spirit to know and together follow Jesus, walk with him and share him. It's an excellent resource for small group leaders because it takes them through the basics of leading in the sequence of three weekends as follows.

☐ Level 1—The Joy of Following Jesus—The basics of spiritual formation and friendship evangelism.

☐ Level 2—The Joy of Bible Discovery—How to study the Bible for yourself and how to prepare and lead studies.

☐ Level 3—The Joy of Growing Together—Vision and tools for disciplemaking.

For more information ask your InterVarsity staff worker or write to Bible & Life at P.O. Box 7895, Madison, WI 53707-7895.

■ *Daily Discovery.* This system for personal inductive Bible study helps you find the central truth in a passage and build that truth into your life. Use this approach for a while, then share it with a friend! To get the most from this study you need: (1) a version of the Bible with paragraphs and (2) a notebook for writing down your findings.

☐ When you open God's Word, expect to meet with him and to learn something about him. Expect to find more of who he is and what he wants you to be like. In a wonderful way you'll grow to understand God and his ways if you approach the Bible open to be changed by what you find there.

☐ Each day as you begin, open your heart to the teaching of the Holy Spirit; ask him to give you understanding and to help you think and act in God's way.

☐ As you conclude a day's study, apply to your life one truth God has shown you as you relate to him.

☐ Do as much of a step as is comfortable each day.

STEP ONE: Book Overview

1. Read it, if it's brief. If it's long, skim it. *If it's a narrative,* jot down a fact about one or two of the main characters; list a few major events. *If it's a letter, note a few facts about the writer and those being addressed. If it's another kind of literature,* list some facts that impress you.

2. Write down a few of your major impressions of the book.

3. What helps do you think you'll get for your life from this book? Write down one or two and ask the Lord to move in your life in these ways.

STEP TWO: The Book (continued)

1. Look through the book to find which chapters can be most naturally grouped together, either by main characters, events or geography. On a simple chart, show the two or three or four major divisions of the book, the natural groups of chapters. Give each division a short title.

2. What seems to be the main theme of the book? Write it in a short sentence over your chart.

3. How does that theme apply to you personally? In what part of your life do you need to act on that truth? Write down a specific way you can begin to do that and ask the Lord to strengthen you in it.

STEP THREE: Chapter or Part of a Chapter

(If your version of the Bible has many short paragraphs, you can group them into thought-units and treat each unit as you would a paragraph.)

1. Make a list of *facts* that you observe in the chapter (or part). Note who, when, what, where and how. Note also any interesting

things about people, places, situations, atmosphere. Include things that are emphasized, like words that are repeated or contrasted. To cover a passage, make just a few observations on each paragraph.

2. Write down your major *impressions* of the passage. What "hits" you from this passage?

3. What does this passage teach about the *Lord?* What difference does it make to you that he is like this? Take some time to praise him.

STEP FOUR: The Chapter or Part (continued)

1. Choose a short *title* for each paragraph.

2. What *connections* can you find between paragraphs? Look for a few, such as repeated words, similarities, contrasts, cause and effect. What significance or *meaning* do you find in each of these connections? Jot down the meanings.

3. Then, look at the meanings, connections and facts and ask yourself: What is the main thing going on in this passage? In other words, what is the *central truth* this passage is teaching? Write that truth in a sentence.

4. What is the main thing the Lord is saying to you through this passage? Here are some possibilities. Select just one.

a. Something to *obey* or an example to follow or avoid? What is it exactly? How can I soon practice it?

b. A *truth about the Lord* I can rejoice in? In what part of my life is this truth especially encouraging?

c. A *promise* I can take for a situation I'm in? Are there conditions in the promise which I need to fulfill? What are they? What does the Lord say he'll do? (Memorizing the promise will help in the days ahead.)

THE NEXT STEP: The Next Chapter or Part

Continue as in step 3, then proceed as in step 4. *Move along at your own pace.*

THE FINAL STEP

When you finish studying the chapters, notice how their main truths connect with each other. As you connect these main truths, you are beginning to put together the *teaching* of the Bible. See if from these you can write the *theme of the book* in a sentence. How does it fit with the theme you saw at first? Share these with a Christian friend or group studying the same book. See how your theme compares with that in a Bible handbook.

■ *Ordering manuscripts of biblical texts.* Manuscript versions of the following biblical texts are available through InterVarsity Christian Fellowship of Southern California. All texts are from the Revised Standard Version and are used by permission.

	Text	Price		Text	Price
_____	Genesis 1—3*	$ .60	_____	Luke	$3.75
_____	Genesis 1—11	1.45	_____	John	3.50
_____	Exodus	4.00	_____	John 1—4*	.70
_____	Exodus 32—34*	.60	_____	John 14—17*	.60
_____	Joshua	3.50	_____	Acts	4.00
_____	Ruth	.60	_____	Romans	2.00
_____	Nehemiah	2.75	_____	Romans 1—8*	1.00
_____	Esther	1.20	_____	1 Corinthians	1.75
_____	Ecclesiastes	1.20	_____	2 Corinthians	1.30
_____	Isaiah 1—12	1.75	_____	Galatians	.70
_____	Isaiah 40—55	2.75	_____	Ephesians	.70
_____	Daniel	2.75	_____	Philippians	.60
_____	Hosea	2.40	_____	Colossians	.50
_____	Amos	1.30	_____	1 Thessalonians	.50
_____	Jonah	.30	_____	1 Timothy	.60
_____	Micah	1.20	_____	2 Timothy	.50
_____	Nahum	.60	_____	Titus	.30
_____	Habakkuk	.60	_____	Philemon	1.50
_____	Haggai	.30	_____	Hebrews	1.50
_____	Malachi	.50	_____	James	1.50
_____	Matthew	3.50	_____	1 Peter	.60
_____	Matthew 5—7*	.75	_____	1 John	.60
_____	Mark	3.00	_____	Revelation	2.00
_____	Mark 1—4*	.75			

_____ Send one of each [except those marked with an *] 50.00

_____ Manuscript Teaching Guide 4.00

_____ Send order forms. I need this order by: _____________________

Please allow *10-14* days for delivery. Large orders and orders outside of the continental United States will take longer. Please place your order with this time frame in mind in order to avoid disappointments. We are especially busy at the beginning of the fall, winter and summer quarters. Indicate the quantity needed of each below (permission is granted to photocopy this list).

Most orders will be sent by UPS unless otherwise requested. Please do not use a P.O. Box for the shipping address. You will be billed for the cost of the manuscripts plus shipping charges, a handling charge of $1.00 per order, and applicable sales tax. *Please withhold payment until billed.* Send to: IVCF Manuscript Service, P.O. Box 40250, Pasadena, CA 91114-7250 or call (818) 449-0522.

Bible Study Guides from InterVarsity Press

■ *Caring People Bible Studies.* Seven guides by Phyllis J. Le Peau and an introductory handbook cover all the basics of caregiving, as well as helping people work through these areas of their own lives. Each guide includes eight or nine studies: *Caring for Emotional Needs, Caring for People in Conflict, Caring for People in Grief, Caring for Physical Needs, Caring for Spiritual Needs, The Character of Caring People, Handbook for Caring People* and *Resources for Caring People.*

■ *Christian Basics Bible Studies.* Christian Basics are the keys to becoming a mature disciple. The six studies in each of these guides, based on some well-loved books, will take you through key Scripture passages and help you to apply biblical truths to your life. The guides are *Certainty: Know Why You Believe* by Paul Little with Scott Hotaling, *Character: Who You Are When No One's Looking* by Bill Hybels, *Christ: Basic Christianity* by John Stott, *Commitment: My Heart—Christ's Home* by Robert Boyd Munger, *Christ's Body: The Community of the King* by Howard Snyder, *Decisions: Finding God's Will* by J. I. Packer, *Excellence: Run with the Horses* by Eugene Peterson, *Lordship: Basic Discipleship* by Floyd McClung, *Perseverance: A Long Obedience in the Same Direction* by Eugene Peterson, *Prayer: Too Busy Not to Pray* by Bill Hybels, *Priorities: Tyranny of the Urgent* by Charles Hummel, *Scripture: God's Word for Contemporary Christians* by John Stott, *Spiritual Warfare: The Fight* by John White, *Witnessing:*

How to Give Away Your Faith by Paul Little with Dale and Sandy Larsen, *Work: Serving God by What We Do* by Ben Patterson and *Worship: Serving God with Our Praise* by Ben Patterson.

■ *Christian Character Bible Studies.* Designed to help grow godly lives, each guide features an adaptable length format for six or twelve studies, notes on difficult passages, tips on small group dynamics and extra help for leaders. The series includes *Deciding Wisely, Staying Faithful, Finding Contentment, Living in the World, Loving God, Loving One Another, Loving the World* and *Pursuing Holiness.*

■ *Created Male and Female Bible Studies.* This series, by Cindy Bunch, Brian Wallace and Scott Hotaling, is designed to help groups and individuals discover what it means that we are created in God's image—male and female. Some guides are for women's groups, some for men's groups and some for mixed groups. Twelve studies are in each: *Created Female, Created Male, Created for Relationships, Following God Together, Men Facing Temptation, Roles in Ministry, Sexual Wholeness* and *Women Facing Temptation.*

■ *Life Recovery Guides.* Bringing biblical principles to life in a powerful way, Dale and Juanita Ryan provide help for people dealing with pain. Each guide includes six studies: *Recovery: A Lifelong Journey* (Steps 10-12), *Recovery from Abuse, Recovery from Addictions,* (Steps 1-3) *Recovery from Bitterness, Recovery from Broken Relationships, Recovery from Codependency, Recovery from Depression, Recovery from Distorted Images of God, Recovery from Distorted Images of Self, Recovery from Family Dysfunctions, Recovery from Fear, Recovery from Guilt* (Steps 4-9), *Recovery from Loss, Recovery from Shame, Recovery from Spiritual Abuse* and *Recovery from Workaholism.*

■ *LifeGuide® Bible Studies.* LifeGuides are inductive studies designed to take forty-five to sixty minutes to complete in a group. Each guide has leader's notes at the back. If you are leading a new group you might want to begin with a book study of a Gospel, like Mark or John, or one of the shorter letters, like Ephesians.

☐ Topical Studies

Angels/12 studies by Douglas Connelly, *Christian Beliefs*/12 studies by Stephen Eyre, *Christian Character*/12 studies by Andrea Sterk & Peter Scazzero, *Christian Community*/12 studies by Rob Suggs, *Chris-*

tian Disciplines/12 studies by Andrea Sterk & Peter Scazzero, *Christian Virtues*/10 studies by Cindy Bunch & Scott Hotaling, *David*/12 studies by Jack Kuhatschek, *End Times*/13 studies by Paul Stevens, *Evangelism*/12 studies by Rebecca Pippert & Ruth Siemens, *Friendship*/12 studies by Carolyn Nystrom, *Fruit of the Spirit*/9 studies by Hazel Offner, *Jesus, the Reason*/11 studies by James W. Sire, *Loving Justice*/12 studies by Bob & Carol Hunter, *Marriage*/12 studies by James & Martha Reapsome, *Mary*/10 studies by Douglas & Karen Connelly, *Meeting God*/12 studies by J. I. Packer, *Meeting Jesus*/13 studies by Leighton Ford, *Meeting the Spirit*/12 studies by Douglas Connelly, *New Testament Characters*/12 studies by Carolyn Nystrom, *Old Testament Characters*/12 studies by Peter Scazzero, *Old Testament Kings*/12 studies by Carolyn Nystrom, *Parables*/12 studies by John White, *Prayer*/12 studies by David Healey, *Self-Esteem*/9 studies by Jack Kuhatschek, *Sermon on the Mount*/13 studies by John Stott, *Small Group Starter Kit*/6 studies for groups by Jeffrey Arnold, *Spiritual Gifts*/12 studies by Charles & Anne Hummel, *Suffering*/11 studies by Jack Kuhatshek, *Women of the New Testament*/12 studies by Phyllis J. Le Peau, and *Women of the Old Testament*/12 studies by Gladys Hunt.

☐ Small Group Books

Leading Bible Discussions (rev.)/by James F. Nyquist & Jack Kuhatschek and *Starting (& Ending) a Small Group*/by Dan Williams.

☐ Old Testament Books

Genesis/26 studies by Charles & Anne Hummel, *Exodus*/24 studies by James Reapsome, *Joshua*/12 studies by Donald Baker, *Judges*/12 studies by Donald Baker, *Nehemiah*/13 studies by Don Fields, *Esther*/9 studies by Patty Pell, *Job*/12 studies by Paul Stevens, *Psalms*/12 studies by Eugene H. Peterson, *Psalms II*/12 studies by Juanita Ryan, *Proverbs*/13 studies by William Mouser, *Ecclesiastes*/12 studies by Bill and Teresa Syrios, *Isaiah*/24 studies by Howard Peskett, *Jeremiah*/12 studies by Stephen Eyre, *Daniel*/12 studies by Douglas Connelly, *Hosea*/12 studies by Dale and Sandy Larsen and *Jonah, Joel & Amos*/13 studies by Doug & Doris Haugen.

☐ New Testament Books

Matthew/24 studies by Stephen & Jacalyn Eyre, *Mark*/22 studies by

James Hoover, *Luke*/26 studies by Ada Lum, *John*/26 studies by Douglas Connelly, *Acts*/24 studies by Phyllis J. Le Peau, *Romans*/21 studies by Jack Kuhatschek, *1 Corinthians*/13 studies by Paul Stevens & Dan Williams, *2 Corinthians*/12 studies by Paul Stevens, *Galatians*/12 studies by Jack Kuhatschek, *Ephesians*/13 studies by Andrew T. & Phyllis J. Le Peau, *Philippians*/9 studies by Donald Baker, *Colossians & Philemon*/10 studies by Martha Reapsome, *1 & 2 Thessalonians*/11 studies by Donald Baker, *1 & 2 Timothy and Titus*/12 studies by Pete Sommer, *Hebrews*/13 studies by James Reapsome, *James*/11 studies by Andrew T. & Phyllis J. Le Peau, *1 & 2 Peter and Jude*/12 studies by Carolyn Nystrom, *John's Letters*/13 studies by Ron Blankley and *Revelation*/12 studies by Paul Stevens.

Books on Nurture

Arnold, Jeffrey. *Discovering the Bible for Yourself.* Downers Grove, Ill.: InterVarsity Press, 1993. A step-by-step handbook that walks groups and individuals through doing an inductive Bible study.

Blomberg, Craig L. *The Historical Reliability of the Gospels.* Downers Grove, Ill.: InterVarsity Press, 1987. A strong comprehensive case for the consistency and reliability of Scripture.

Bruce, F. F. *The Canon of Scripture.* Downers Grove, Ill.: InterVarsity Press, 1988. Historical evidence for the acceptance of the canon.

Guthrie, Donald, ed. *New Bible Dictionary,* 2nd edition. Downers Grove, Ill.: InterVarsity Press, 1991. Comprehensive coverage of books, people, places, terms, doctrines, history, geography, customs and current issues in archaeology and biblical studies.

Keener, Craig. *The IVP Bible Background Commentary: New Testament.* Downers Grove, Ill.: InterVarsity Press, 1993. Useful information on the historical and cultural backgrounds of nearly every verse in the New Testament.

Stuart, Douglas, and Gordon D. Fee. *How to Read the Bible for All Its Worth.* Grand Rapids, Mich.: Zondervan, 1993. The basics of good Bible reading and study.

Wenham, G. J., et al., ed. *New Bible Commentary,* 4th edition. Downers Grove, Ill.: InterVarsity Press, 1994. Solid, concise commentaries on every book of the Bible.

4
OUTREACH RESOURCES

AGGRESSIVE OUTREACH

Taken from *It Came from Beneath the Pew* by Rob Suggs (Downers Grove, Ill.: InterVarsity Press, 1991) and used by permission.

This chapter is divided into a number of sections. The first part contains general ideas appropriate for outreach in a number of areas. The next section is focused on reaching seekers with the gospel, and many of these ideas have a particular campus focus. The third section is about world mission, and the fourth deals with social action. The books at the end deal with each of these areas.

■ *Dreams about mission.* After your group has decided how it will reach out to others, use this exercise in planning.

1. Identifying the people.
   a. Who are they?
   b. Where are they?
   c. What are their major interests?
   d. What barriers stand in the way of their hearing the gospel? Of their understanding and responding?
   e. What is their greatest felt need? How could we help meet that need?
2. Praying for the people.
   a. List ways you can pray for these people.
   b. Discuss ways you may be used as answers to those prayers.
   c. Take action accordingly.
3. Involving ourselves with them.
   a. With the Lord's help, what would we like to see happen in their lives?
   b. What are some ways to involve ourselves in this?
   c. What materials do we need for this?
   d. Do we need further training? What? When? Where?
   e. What prayer requests for ourselves do we make before God?

■ *Invite a speaker.* James W. Sire, author of *The Universe Next Door* and *Why Should Anyone Believe Anything at All?* is currently available to speak on campuses and in churches. He specializes in evangelistic lectures and discussions, discipleship training, lectures in comparative religion and philosophy, public dialogues with proponents of views that counter Christianity, and lectures or sermons on the Gospels. Topics that Dr. Sire has lectured on include

Why Should Anyone Believe Anything at All?

Jesus the Reason

Will the Real God (If Any) Please Stand Up?
Are the Gospels Historically Reliable?
An Introduction to the New Age Movement
Developing a Christian Mind
Scripture Twisting
Engaging the University.

He is also senior editor at InterVarsity Press and can be contacted there: P.O. Box 1400, Downers Grove, IL 60515 (708) 887-2500.

■ *Pray.*

☐ For areas of your community and groups that have not been reached with the gospel.

☐ For opportunities to begin sharing the gospel with friends who do not believe in Jesus Christ as Savior and Lord.

☐ For short- and long-term missionaries from your church or fellowship.

☐ For IVCF execs or church leadership teams.

☐ For issues in the newspaper and countries affected.

☐ For different parts of the world—one week pray for Eastern Europe, the next Africa and so on. *Operation World,* MARC's unreached people prayer guides (919 West Huntington Drive, Monrovia, CA 91016) and 10/40 Window prayer cards (Caleb Project, 10 West Dry Creek Circle, Littleton, CO 80120) are possible resources for prayer requests.

☐ For people you know around the world—concentrate on Europe and pray for all those you know involved in ministry there. Next week concentrate on the Middle East, then on Oceania and so on.

■ *Show to tell.*

☐ In a busy parking lot wash car windows for free and leave a little note saying you are part of a small group and tell where it meets. (Patty Pell)

☐ Focus your outreach to freshmen during orientation week through setting up booktables (have brochures about IVCF available) at activities fairs, hosting dorm discussions, sponsoring fun events like movies, dances, picnics and volleyball games, helping new students move into dorms and apartments or doing a door-to-door welcome.

- ☐ After studying the parable of the Great Banquet it is fun to prepare your own banquet, which can be as simple as investing in a lot of pizza. Have an open dinner at church or in the dorm and invite everyone that you see to come and enjoy the feast with you. (Sue Sage)
- ☐ For early risers: make a couple of dozen muffins and a couple of containers of juice and place those in an easily accessible place for people to enjoy. (Sue Sage)
- ☐ Distribute care packages during finals or at some other high stress time. You can include fruit, aspirin, cough drops, blue books and #2 pencils, crazy stress-relief toys like those bouncy balls, cookies, granola bars or tea—anything that is conducive to study or stress relief. (Sue Sage)
- ☐ Be a mystery! Find a way to do something simple for people as a practical example of God's love for them—no strings attached! By doing this you'll make your church or organization more visible and give a taste of grace. For example, here's a plan for cleaning dorm rooms as a small group:
    1. Make teams of two to cover a floor or series of suites (make sure someone on your team actually lives in the dorm) during a time when students are there.
    2. Choose a bunch of things you can offer (for example, sweeping the floor, making a bed, cleaning windows, cleaning a computer screen [yes, this has been popular!] and anything else you can come up with). Make up a sheet to hand to people explaining who you are, what you're offering and why.

Choose One: (FREE!)

☐ sweep your floor

☐ clean your computer screen

☐ make your bed

☐ wash your windows

This is a practical example of God's love for you.

From IVCF

3. Gather necessary materials (brooms, dustpans, vacuum cleaner, Windex, paper towels)
4. Greet the students in their rooms, saying, "Hi! Choose one!" Let the student check one and return it to you. If you're talkative, you can explain yourself. If not, just point to the answers on the sheet. The only thing you have to be emphatic about is that you really want to sweep their floors.
5. Afterward, you may want to leave a little note, invitation to a small group, or even a calling card.
6. At the end get together, share your experiences and pray for the people you served.
7. Work at continuing contact with the people you served.

This works well as a one-time event, a regular missions activity, or as a spark for growing your small group or starting an evangelistic group. It's great for people who are scared to share their faith. (Allen Lincoln)

■ *Skit night* by Marsha Petty, Penn. Spend one small group session working on a skit to present for a large group or a church meeting to inspire others to get involved in outreach. Or create a skit to reach seekers and perform in a public area. Make the planning session a party and a break from the group's routine. Plan and practice a skit together, then have pizza or donuts. This is a great community builder.

■ *Study.* Circulate materials on evangelism, social issues or world missions in your small group—*Rich Christians in an Age of Hunger* (Word), *Out of the Saltshaker* (IVP), *Speaking of Jesus* (IVP) and a number of materials available through IVCF Missions, P.O. Box 7895, Madison, WI 53707.

■ *Train.*

☐ Attend a missions or evangelism conference as a small group (such as Urbana).

☐ Contact Discover the World (3244 E. Orange Grove Blvd., Pasadena, CA 91107) for church-oriented training programs to equip and mobilize members for missions. Contact Global Opportunities (1600 Elizabeth St., Pasadena, CA 91104) for semi-

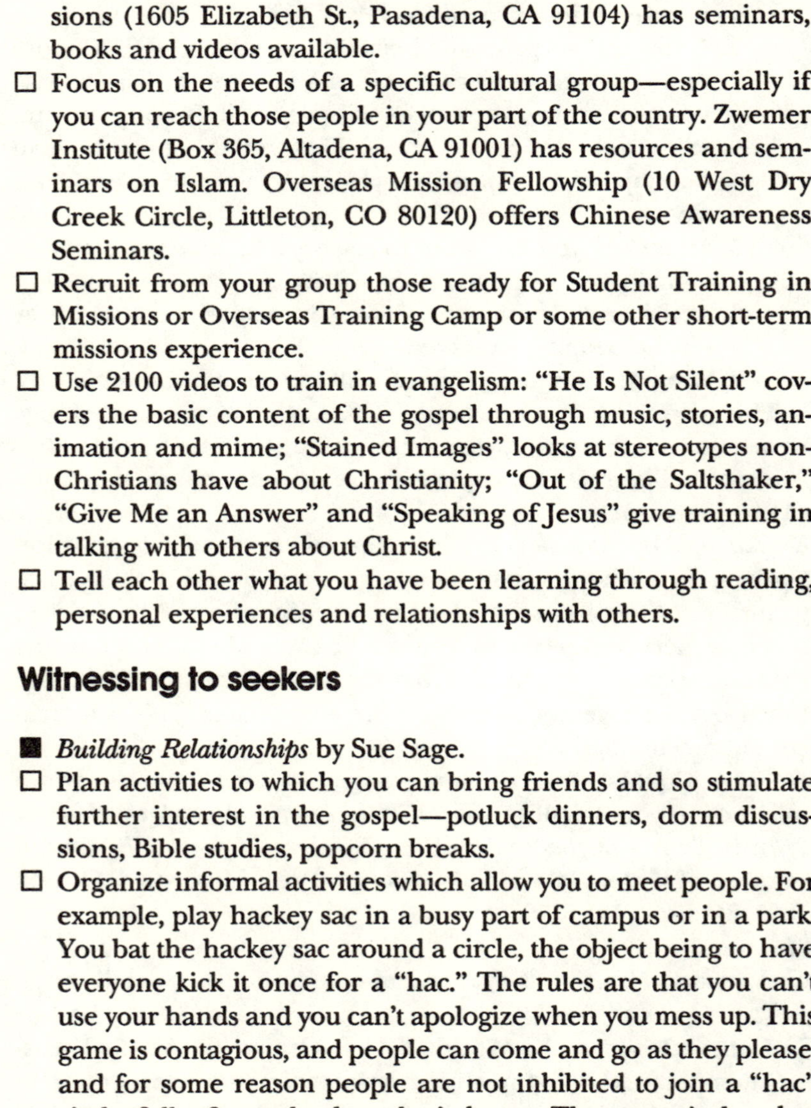

nars and resources on tentmaking. US Center for World Missions (1605 Elizabeth St., Pasadena, CA 91104) has seminars, books and videos available.

- ☐ Focus on the needs of a specific cultural group—especially if you can reach those people in your part of the country. Zwemer Institute (Box 365, Altadena, CA 91001) has resources and seminars on Islam. Overseas Mission Fellowship (10 West Dry Creek Circle, Littleton, CO 80120) offers Chinese Awareness Seminars.
- ☐ Recruit from your group those ready for Student Training in Missions or Overseas Training Camp or some other short-term missions experience.
- ☐ Use 2100 videos to train in evangelism: "He Is Not Silent" covers the basic content of the gospel through music, stories, animation and mime; "Stained Images" looks at stereotypes non-Christians have about Christianity; "Out of the Saltshaker," "Give Me an Answer" and "Speaking of Jesus" give training in talking with others about Christ.
- ☐ Tell each other what you have been learning through reading, personal experiences and relationships with others.

Witnessing to seekers

- ■ *Building Relationships* by Sue Sage.
- ☐ Plan activities to which you can bring friends and so stimulate further interest in the gospel—potluck dinners, dorm discussions, Bible studies, popcorn breaks.
- ☐ Organize informal activities which allow you to meet people. For example, play hackey sac in a busy part of campus or in a park. You bat the hackey sac around a circle, the object being to have everyone kick it once for a "hac." The rules are that you can't use your hands and you can't apologize when you mess up. This game is contagious, and people can come and go as they please, and for some reason people are not inhibited to join a "hac" circle full of people they don't know. The sport is low key enough that you can get to know people while playing.

- ☐ Sit in the cafeteria during lunches when many people come and go quickly. Set aside an hour for lunch with the main goal being not only to get some food, but also to sit with as many people that you don't know as possible.

■ *Christianeze self-help* by Nairy Ohanian. This is a revealing activity that helps in communicating the gospel. Bring stacks of 3 × 5 index cards (preferably white). Have the group brainstorm all their favorite Christian lingo, spiritual buzzwords and overused church words. Examples that will arise: *salvation, grace, sanctified, holy.* But also include words as *fellowship, church, Scriptures, worship* and *share.*

Write the words on the blank side of the index cards. Now have group members write alternative words, which define these terms, on the lined side of the card. The goal is to learn and use words which share truth in a simple, relevant way for our nonspiritual friends. For example, for "grace" you might have: *Gift, freebie, money can't buy, undeserved good thing.* Or for "fellowship": *gathering of people, celebration, meeting with Christians.*

Have each member make their own packet of cards. Then quiz one another. Encourage everyone to carry their cards with them, learn alternative words and practice sharing the gospel without Christianeze!

■ *Coffee talks* by Nina Thiel. Small group members go around their dorm with video cameras and interview their hallmates on camera, asking, "When you hear the name Jesus, what do you think?" and "How would you describe your spiritual life?"

A week or so later, the video (having been edited) is shown at a coffeehouse set up in the dorm lounge. The group gets card tables, tablecloths, mugs and good coffee. Small groups from off-campus bake and bring really nice desserts, and serve the people. Small group members all sit at different tables, and after the video is shown, they initiate conversations about the spiritual issues that came up in the video.

■ *Don't forget to share your faith!* by Mike Ortiz and Dale Brady, N.Y. Here's an idea for those who want to speak to others about Christ but don't know where (or how) to start. Each member ties a string around a finger where it could be easily seen, making a commitment to leave it on for twenty-four hours. Inevitably, others will ask what it's for. You can decide prior to the activity what your response will be. Perhaps to "be thankful for all God has given you" or "to pray for a friend." But the hope is also to start a conversation that will help you identify yourself as a Christian and possibly ask others about their thoughts on spiritual issues. This is a simple way to be identified with Christ and allow him to open up some exciting conversations. When you return to your group the following week, there will be plenty of stories to tell.

■ *Door-to-door visits* by Brian Parks, Ky. Spend a small group meeting reaching out to the dorm or neighborhood where you meet. Pair up and go door-to-door telling people about the group and inviting them to come sometime. If there's openness, the gospel can be shared. Another idea is to go door-to-door just asking for prayer requests. The pairs explain that they are Christians and that part of being a Christian is praying for the people around them. Praying for them on the spot is ideal, or leaving, praying and following up later works too.

■ *The empty chair* by Lyman Coleman, Colo. Set up an extra chair for each group meeting and pray for God to fill that chair with a new person. This will help the group keep an attitude of openness to visitors and give members the freedom to invite non-Christian friends.

■ *Evangelism time line* by Kelle Ashton. Here's a plan for making evangelism a part of your campus or church group for a year. This will help you to build a vision for outreach into the group from the start, rather than trying to add it in later.

A. Now and Summer
   1. Pray for Christians who will be in your group to have an evangelistic attitude.
   2. Pray for non-Christians to be involved in your group.

B. September
   1. Keep praying.
   2. Meet as many people as possible. Fall is a key time to make connections with new students on campus and is a time

when churches have many new visitors.

3. Invite people to your small group.
4. If you are assigned members by a small group coordinator, meet with them individually. Early in the relationship, you'll probably get a sense of whether they're Christians or not. Be open and honest, and usually they will too.
5. Encourage group members to bring friends.
6. Introduce 2 PLUS plan (see p. 105) and begin praying for non-Christian friends during small group prayer times.

C. October and November
1. If your church or fellowship offers a retreat or evangelism training session, encourage your whole group to attend together.
2. Organize a fun, nonthreatening activity for your group to do as a whole and to invite your 2 PLUS people to.

D. December and January
Support one another in inviting your 2 PLUS people to church or a fellowship meeting or a winter retreat.

E. February
1. If available, as a group activity, go to an investigative Bible discussion training together. If training is not available, the brief book *Introducing Jesus* by Pete Scazzero will give you background and studies to use in a seeker's group. There are also some tips for leading an investigative group on page 101.
2. Challenge one another to ask 2 PLUS people to be in an investigative Bible discussion or seeker's group. You may want to actually have these new people join your group and use appropriate material or hold a short-term group at another time.

F. March
1. Keep praying for 2 PLUS people and the investigative Bible discussion.
2. Consider doing an outreach project as a group during spring vacation. For example, you could join a beach evangelism project or work with Habitat for Humanity.

G. April

Encourage one another to explain to the 2 PLUS people who are ready what it means to commit their lives to Christ.

■ *Evangelistic parties.* In a fun, relaxed, relational and informal setting seekers feel more free to express their thoughts and feelings about the claims of Christ. Here are some guidelines for throwing a great evangelistic party.

1. Develop a strategy of using parties to reach out. In your small group look at Scripture for principles on hospitality and relationships. Discuss the party scene in your community or on your campus. Talk about what makes a good party.

2. Decide what you want to do. Capitalize on creativity. Talk about why you want to throw a party and who it's for.

3. Plan the party. Consider where it will take place, how much it will cost, what kind of theme and decorations you'll have, how you'll get the word out, what kind of food you'll have, what kinds of activities you'll have and how both introverts and extroverts will be made comfortable, and who will clean up.

4. Pray for the party.

5. Have the party. Remember to watch the noise, end at a reasonable hour and have fun.

6. Evaluate the party.

■ *First steps to God.* The following is an outline of the Christian message that was developed for IVCF. It is a useful summary to keep in mind as you share your faith. You may want to keep a copy inside your Bible. You can help each other learn it as a small group. Challenge each other to learn a line or a section each week and report in during small group.

☐ God

A. God loves you (John 3:16).

B. God is holy and just. He punishes all evil and expels it from his presence (Romans 1:18).

☐ Humanity

A. God, who created everything, made us for himself to find our purpose in fellowship with him (Colossians 1:16).

B. But we rebelled and turned away from God (Isaiah 53:6). The result is separation from God (Isaiah 59:2). The penalty is eternal death (Romans 6:23).

☐ Christ

A. God became a man in the person of Jesus Christ to restore the broken fellowship (Colossians 1:19-20). Christ lived a perfect life (1 Peter 2:22).

B. Christ died as a substitute for us by paying the death penalty for our rebellion (Romans 5:8). He arose (1 Corinthians 15:3-4) and is alive today to give us a new life of fellowship with God, now and forever (John 10:10).

☐ Response

A. I must *repent* for my rebellion (Matthew 4:17).

B. I must *believe* Christ died to provide forgiveness and a new life of fellowship with God (John 1:12).

C. I must *receive* Christ as my Savior and Lord with the intent to obey him. I do this in prayer by inviting him into my life (Revelation 3:20).

☐ Cost

A. Cost to God (1 Peter 1:18-19).

B. No cost to you: your salvation (Ephesians 2:8-9).

C. Cost to you: discipleship (Luke 9:23-24).

■ *Following up—a role play* by Ann Beyerlein. You may be unsure about where some group members are with Jesus. What they say in small group gives some idea, but sometimes it is important to follow up their comments and talk to them one-to-one about what they are thinking about spiritual issues. Sometimes the conversation will surprise the leader and can help solidify something in the mind of the member. This can move the member a step closer to becoming a Christian or spur the member on toward spiritual growth.

The leader might just stop by and see a member or ask a member to get together to talk about small group and how things are going spiritually. The leader needs to be ready with a few questions. Beginning with a general question about small group or a question that follows up a comment at small group can be a great way to start. If the person is open, ask about his religious background, what has been significant for her in small group, what he thinks a Christian is, whether she considers herself a Christian or what the barriers are to his becoming a Christian. Ask about her spiritual questions or needs. If the person is obviously a Christian, ask about his spiritual growing edge and what he needs to go deeper.

The following role play for small group leaders will give practice in asking spiritual questions. It can also be used in a small group of Christians to help people practice talking to others about their faith. The small group members listed are all at different places spiritually. The leader has noticed that all are holding back some in small group. They may not pray or fully participate. All of these people seem a bit stuck spiritually. The leader prays and decides to have a one-to-one conversation to lovingly ask some questions and see if he or she can help these members become unstuck. This person playing the leader should not know the exact situation of the group member beforehand. The fun is in the discovery.

1. Susie won't pray because she's not sure she is a Christian. She has a lot of doubts about what Christianity is about. She feels some guilt about where she is spiritually.

2. John won't pray because he knows he's not a Christian. He's bothered by the suffering in the world. He has no idea why Jesus died on the cross. He thinks there may be a connection between Jesus' death on the cross and how God feels about suffering.

3. Drake has been coming to small group all year. He'd become a Christian if someone would just ask him and explain to him how to receive Christ.

4. Debbie comes to small group about half of the time. The other half of the time she's having too much fun to show up. She's not sure if she is a Christian. She doesn't feel good about her lifestyle but she doesn't want to give up some of the things she enjoys.

■ *Give a testimony* by Ted McMullen, Ind. Ask someone in your small group to give a testimony for an investigative study or to encourage other small group members. Choose someone who, first of all, is growing and bearing fruit in his or her life. Second, select someone who can stay in the time frame of three to four minutes and can connect with the theme of the Bible study. Let the person know why he or she was chosen. After the testimony is outlined, have the person run through it so that you can make sure it's on track and within the time frame. Help them to avoid "Christianeze." Don't forget to be encouraging.

Here's an outline for a testimony that shows how faith and good works relate: "I decided to trust Christ as Lord of my life when I was [add specifics]. It has been a process of learning how to obey God and serve others [add examples]. I have prioritized faith, but what I do shows that I have made a decision for Christ and belong to him."

Another approach would be for you to interview another Christian during the meeting. You will need to practice together in advance to make sure you keep within the given time frame. Here are some interview questions on the topic of lordship:

1. Tell us a little about your life before you understood what it meant to be a Christian.

2. What were some of your ways of acting and dealing with things, and where did they lead you?

3. When did you begin to understand about having a relationship with Christ?

4. What were some things that held you back from giving Christ control or "lordship" of your life?

5. When did you decide to give control of your life to Christ, and what made you willing to do this?

6. What have you noticed to be different about God now compared to what made you hesitant about him before?

7. How would you summarize the changes that have happened in your life since you gave Christ control?

■ *Guidelines for evangelistic talks* by Doug Whallon, Mass. An evangelistic talk is a meeting convened in a dormitory or hall of residence (sorority, fraternity or club) or some other public place where the claims of Jesus Christ are presented in a short address or testimony. The intent of the talk may be either evangelistic (containing a direct presentation of the gospel of our Lord Jesus Christ) or preevangelistic (focusing on Jesus Christ with the intent of stimulating the listeners to investigate Christ more thoroughly and/or assessing their personal bankruptcy without Christ). The purpose of such talks is twofold: (1) to provide witness to Jesus Christ, and (2) to assist the Christians who live in the residence or community to share Christ by providing a springboard for further conversation.

☐ Suggested Format

1. A word of welcome by a Christian who lives on the floor, and a brief but compelling introduction of the speaker.
2. A fifteen-minute presentation or testimony by the speaker that witnesses to Jesus Christ.
3. A fifteen-minute question and answer period (expect anything).
4. A word of thanks by the initial person, explaining the booklets that are freely available, and how they may be obtained (circulate sign-up list to receive booklets).
5. Prompt dismissal, although further interaction is welcomed.

☐ Who Should Come?

1. Non-Christians living in your dorm or community.
2. Christians who bring with them one or more of their friends who are non-Christians.
3. Young Christians who will grow in faith and confidence as a result.

☐ Topic Selection

1. Be stabbing and thought-provoking
2. Focus on personal needs and problems
3. Be self-explanatory
4. Accurately describe the content (do not be deceptive)
5. Example topics from Larry Thiel, Nev.:
   Would a Good God Send a Good Person to Hell?
   Sex, Drugs and Rock 'n' Roll: Is God Part of the Good Life?
   Christianity on Trial
   Evidence for the Christian Faith
   If God Is So Loving, Why Is the World So Messed Up?
   Death, the Final Frontier (Is There Life After Death?)
   Would Jesus Attend a Frat Party?

☐ The Role of the Sponsoring Small Group

1. Pray as a small group before, during and after the event. Inform others who will pray.

2. Determine a leader who can coordinate the mechanics and help delegate different responsibilities.

3. Gain permission from appropriate authorities to use the lounge or meeting room (usually the RA has this responsibility).

4. Contact and confirm your speaker specifying when, where, what, how long and why.

5. Publicize

   a. One week in advance put up posters describing basic information.

   b. During the last week, invite friends.

   c. Fifteen minutes in advance, remind people by knocking on doors of people on the floor (avoid being obnoxious).

6. Food (soda, juice, popcorn, chips, cookies) encourages people to hang out afterward and ask questions or talk in small clusters.

7. Room organization do's and don'ts (from Larry Thiel): Do have the speaker away from the entrance to the lounge so people will feel comfortable trickling in and out. Don't put the refreshments by the door—the goal is to get people to stick around and get into conversations. Don't have small group members sit together. Do have small group members spread out and sit among the friends they bring. Don't have small group members come up to talk to the speaker after the talk. Do have them talk with the people around them about the talk and the gospel.

8. The day after, have Christians drop off the specified booklets at the rooms of those who indicated a desire for literature; this is a great opportunity to inquire about their reaction and to converse about Christ.

9. Write a thank-you note to the speaker.

■ *If Jesus is the answer, what are the questions?* This self-assessment will help you to be aware of people's needs and how to communicate the gospel.

1. Take time to think about your own life. What are the major questions that you face? Write them down.

2. Think about one or more of your non-Christian friends. What are their major questions about life?

3. Compare your list with those of your friends. Most people doing this exercise find that their own questions are not that different from those of their friends.

4. How has the message of the gospel given you answers to your questions? Think through each question and write down how the gospel is "good news" to you. Think about the questions of your friends. How is the gospel good news to them? How would you communicate this good news in a way that they would understand it?

■ *Interest survey* by Peter Cha, Ill. Small group members survey a dorm, interest group or fraternity on potential dorm talk topics. This can also be a great conversation starter. Here's a sample.

Which questions interest you most? Number your top three.
______ Why do you say that Jesus Christ is the only way to God?
______ Aren't there many ways to God?
______ Isn't it enough to live a good life?
______ Does it matter what you believe as long as you are sincere?
______ How could a loving God send people to Hell?
______ Why do innocent people suffer?
______ Isn't believing in Jesus irrational?
______ Isn't the New Testament full of errors?
______ Why do Christians think they know how other people should live?
______ I'm happy. Why do I need Jesus?
______ ______________________________ (fill in your own question)

yes no
____ ____ Would you be interested in a workshop or discussion group on one of your top three questions?

If yes, leave your name and phone number, and we'll contact you.

Name ______________________ Phone ______________________

■ *Leading an investigative Bible study* by Ada Lum.

☐ Use a modern translation, because it is easier to follow when everyone has the same wording. If you have the same edition, then you can just give the page number. (When not everyone is familiar with the Bible, it is less embarrassing than fumbling around trying to find 1 John.) Make sure you have extra Bibles on hand.

☐ Prepare with a coleader. It really helps. Pray together too!

☐ Set some ground rules for discussion and explain them at the first meeting and whenever a new member joins the group.

☐ Be enthusiastic. Relax.

☐ Don't be uptight about setting doctrine straight as questions or comments raise concerns.

☐ Be excited that they are discovering something from the Bible, even if it's not quite accurate yet.

☐ Avoid answering your own questions. Be comfortable with silences. Remember, they haven't spent the time you have in finding answers to these questions, so they are probably busy looking and thinking.

☐ Pray regularly for your friends that God will open their spiritual understanding and kindle in them an interest and a longing to know him.

☐ Love group members as friends, real people, not souls to be saved. Let them enrich your life, learn from them and affirm them.

☐ Follow through after the study (when it seems appropriate) with some questions that let them know you are interested in them and have been thinking about what they have said or are grappling with. "What have you been learning from the study?" "Have your ideas about God changed since you've been studying the Bible?" Remember, we dare not pressure people. God doesn't barge his way in. So we must follow his example and be sensitive in our inquiries.

Study Questions

These questions can help to bring out the uniqueness and the authority of Jesus as the God-man.

- ☐ In what specific ways does Jesus show his interest in people as individuals? his understanding of their basic human needs and not just outward ones? What does he see in people and their human dilemmas that others apparently do not see? In what ways do his attitudes toward people and their predicaments contrast with those of his contemporaries?
- ☐ What do you learn about human nature from Jesus' viewpoint? What does he command? What does he condemn?
- ☐ What happens when Jesus takes on the problems of his society: corruption, pride, ignorance, evil, cruelty, sickness, materialism? What traditions and prejudices does he come up against in doing so?
- ☐ How does Jesus affect people? Why? How do they affect him? Why? How does he bring out the best in people? How does he affirm their personal worth?
- ☐ What "human interest" details do you observe? What unique aspects of Jesus' personality and character does this event reveal? What fresh insights into his life and mission do you now have?
- ☐ What are the implications of Jesus' life and Word for us today? What practical thing can you do this week to employ the truth you have learned?

These questions are only broad guidelines for your personal study. They need specific rewording for your particular group. For example, if you are studying John 3:1-15, which records Jesus' conversation with the religious aristocrat Nicodemus, you will not want to ask, "How does Jesus show his interest in individuals?" Instead, use a sequence of questions which will precipitate insights: "What did Jesus already know about Nicodemus?" "Look at Jesus' response to Nicodemus's opening statement in verse 2. What hidden question did Jesus apparently see behind it?" "If Jesus could understand Nicodemus so well, what do you think he understands about people today—you, for example?"

Adapted from *How to Begin an Evangelistic Bible Study* by Ada Lum, Downers Grove, Ill.: InterVarsity Press, 1971.

■ *Public talks and debates* by Brian Hossink.

□ Depending on your context, these talks can be as general and nonthreatening as a topic like "What's Wrong with the World Today" to something as confrontational as "How a Loving God Can Send People to Hell." You can focus the talk in one dorm or open it in a public area.

□ Set up a debate between a Christian professor or staff worker and an atheist professor. Planning and care is required to make sure this is run properly, but it can reap many rewards as people see that Christians can and do use their intellect.

■ *Talk about it* by Kelle Ashton. Have each person share their fears about evangelism or any bad experiences with evangelism. Talk about the fears and determine one step each person needs to take to overcome their fears. Then commit to pray for each other's accomplishing their next step and overcoming their fears.

■ *30-day evangelism plan* by Len Andyshak, Kans. Those of us who have become Jesus' disciples have realized that we are to be becoming fishers of humanity and to be going to all the world. However, we often feel our attempts at fishing to be very inadequate, or we simply do no fishing at all. It has been well said that one learns fishing only by fishing. This experience is designed to help you get started. It is simple enough to be done by anyone, practical enough to actually produce some changes and stretching enough to keep you depending on the Lord and reminded that this whole process is absolutely miraculous and not contingent upon your limited abilities and strength. You can follow this plan as a small group, offering each other encouragement and accountability along the way. Each week you can talk and pray about what you are learning.

To say it simply, seven things are involved over thirty days. (If you would feel more biblical and assured we could make it seven things and forty days.) One small group member can create a chart of all the activities for each member of the group to use, checking them off each day.

1. Daily prayer. Start each day with a simple, specific prayer something like this: "Here I am, Lord; please heal me, strengthen

me, introduce me to the people you want me to love, and please give me opportunities to share with them about you. Amen."

2. Daily reading. During the thirty days read a book—about five pages a day. (Done daily it provides continued input and encouragement and never becomes a burden.) Two good options are *Speaking of Jesus* by Mack Stiles or *Out of the Saltshaker* by Rebecca Pippert (both IVP).

3. Meeting people. Over the thirty days introduce yourself to fifteen to twenty new people. This can be done anywhere or in any way the Lord leads in answer to that prayer you prayed. Perhaps sitting by someone in class, saying hello and getting their name. Perhaps at a meal, in the shower, running, in the store. Who knows what the Lord may do! Record the names of the people you meet on your chart and review them daily so you don't forget them (a deadly sin in evangelism).

4. Casual time. Four times during the month (once a week) spend some time with a non-Christian friend or acquaintance. It could be the same person each time or four different people. Possibly it will be one of the fifteen to twenty new people you have met. This should be a casual, nonreligious activity of some kind—have a latté, go to a funny movie, study together, go to a party or go roller-blading. Record what you did on your chart.

5. Invitations. Four other times (once a week again) invite one of your non-Christian friends to a "religious" activity. They don't have to accept, you just have to invite them! The invitation could be to church, a Bible study or an evangelistic dorm talk. You could even be daring and invite them to look at Jesus in the Bible with you for a few weeks (but beware of this type of boldness: you never know what might happen—to you or them!).

6. Ask about Jesus. Twice you will simply ask a person what they think about Jesus. You might start by first asking about their church background and if they are still involved. Then move to the question of Jesus. It will get you to the heart of the matter quickly and easily. You will find people surprisingly open with you, especially after having established even a brief friendship with you before this point. As always the key is to be sensitive to the Lord's

guidance—the right person (perhaps not the one you expected) at the right time (perhaps at an inconvenient time or when you are sure you're not ready yet). Remember that simple prayer—he will hear, and he will answer. You can *expect* some miraculous opportunities and the wisdom from above in that moment. " 'Not by might, nor by power, but by my Spirit,' says the LORD" (Zechariah 4:6).

7. Unlimited possibilities. At the end of the thirty days, choose one to three specific goals to continue your evangelistic momentum in the immediate future. The possibilities include 2 PLUS evangelism, a one-to-one evangelistic Bible discussion or joining a club to meet non-Christians. Each small group member should do this, and the group can continue to encourage each other to follow through on their commitments.

(Taken from *A Thirty-Day Evangelism Plan* by Len Andyshak [Downers Grove, Ill.: InterVarsity Press], 1986.)

■ *2 PLUS evangelism.* My commitment to pray consistently for the conversion of two friends and for boldness in taking opportunity to witness to them.

Steps to Live Out 2 PLUS

☐ Acknowledge dependence on God's grace to draw your friends to Christ.
☐ Identify two not-yet Christians for whom you will pray.
☐ Develop a friendship with them.
☐ Choose a prayer partner and pray together for your friends.

While I pray, I build my friendship through:

☐ Spending weekly time with them.
☐ Learning more about them: sports, hobbies, major, arts, experience with other Christians, beliefs about Christ.
☐ Looking for ways to serve them.
☐ Taking risks by inviting them to Bible study, chapter meeting, read a Christian book, church, social events.
☐ Sharing the Gospel with them.

I will pray for: (list names)

1. ______________________________
2. ______________________________

My prayer partner is ______________________________.

My next step(s) to live out 2 PLUS are ______________________.

■ *Using film, video and TV in evangelism.* The media can provide an excellent catalyst for discussion in a variety of settings. Here is a partial list of videos which are good discussion starters. Use the whole film or just a segment, allowing time afterward for discussion. Preview any video you intend to use (don't just rely on your memory). This will help you to formulate discussion questions and allow you to anticipate any scenes that are inappropriate for your intended audience. What may seem like innocent sex scenes to some may be too arousing for others.

Films You May Want to Use

Babbette's Feast (G)—Story of a Parisian refugee who goes to live with two spinster daughters of a minister in a small Danish village. Themes of servanthood, joy and celebration. (1987, Danish)

Broadcast News (R)—Focuses on the TV news world and relationship between three characters. Brings up a variety of issues including ethics and friendship. (1987)

Chariots of Fire (PG)—Story of two men who run in the 1924 Olympics. Contains themes relating to the tension between Christian and secular values and motivations. (1981)

Crimes and Misdemeanors (PG-13)—A Woody Allen film that weaves two different but related stories together. Themes of betrayal, trust, morality, guilt. (1989)

Cry Freedom (PG)—Story about a South African activist's friendship with a newspaper editor. Themes of racism, social justice. (1987)

Dead Poets Society (PG)—Story of an English teacher and his prep school students. Themes include purpose and motivation in life, individualism versus conformity and authority issues. (1989)

Driving Miss Daisy (PG)—Relationship between a cantankerous older woman and her chauffeur. Themes of loyalty, friendship, racism, old age. (1989)

Field of Dreams (PG-13)—Story of a farmer who ends up building a baseball diamond on his property. Themes of faith, reconciliation, hope, family. (1989)

Fried Green Tomatoes (PG-13)—Two stories—one of life in a small southern town and the other of a relationship between two women. Themes of friendship, aging, among others. (1991)

Grand Canyon (R)—Focuses on several interrelated lives and the issues each is facing and how they respond to traumatic events in each of their lives. (1991)

Jesus of Montreal (R)—A group of actors come together for a production of the Passion Play. Themes of religious hypocrisy and commercialism, among others. (1989, French Canadian)

The Mission (PG)—Follows a Jesuit mission in the Brazilian jungle. Issues relating to crosscultural missions, true faith, justice. (1986)

Mosquito Coast (PG)—Idealistic inventor moves his family to a remote South American village where he attempts to play God. Issues of crossing cultures, control, family. (1986)

Places in the Heart (PG)—A widow determined to survive as a farmer takes in boarders. Deals with racism, poverty, death. (1984)

Say Anything (PG-13)—A loner in high school goes after the class brain and is surprised by what he finds. Themes of friendship, betrayal, self-image.

Stand by Me (R)—Friendship between four boys. Themes of friendship, community. (1986)

The Trip to Bountiful (PG)—Story of an elderly woman who longs to see her childhood home. Themes of Christian faith, valuing people. (1985)

Tucker (PG)—True story of an entrepreneurial carmaker in the 1940s who is squeezed out by other carmakers. Issues of integrity, success, failure, business ethics. (1988)

Wall Street (R)—Young hotshot enters the world of Wall Street. Themes of greed, compromise, ethics, family loyalty. (1987)

Here are some questions you can use to discern the underlying values of a TV show or film. For more information see *Movies in Close Up* by Alan MacDonald (Downers Grove, Ill.: InterVarsity Press, 1992).

☐ What is the premise of the movie? Does it agree or conflict with

biblical truth?
- ☐ Who are the heroes? Who are the villains? Who are the Christians and/or religious characters in the film?
- ☐ How is the world portrayed? the government? evil?
- ☐ How is reality portrayed? What are the worldviews of the characters?
- ☐ How is love portrayed? the family?
- ☐ Would you be embarrassed (or offended) to sit through the movie with your parents or Jesus?
- ☐ What are the redemptive elements in the film, and are they enough to offset the destructive elements?

World mission

■ *Books for the world.* Collect used Christian books, videos, Bibles and magazines from chapter members and send them overseas for students in English-speaking IFES movements who have few resources of their own. To find out what countries have requested books, contact IFES World Headquarters, 55 Palmerston Road, Harrow, Middlesex HA3 7RR, England.

■ *Give.* Offer financial support to
- ☐ students from your chapter on global projects or church members going on short-term missions projects.
- ☐ an IFES staffworker or IFES twinning partner (contact IFES—IV-Link, P.O. Box 7895, Madison, WI 53707).
- ☐ a minority IVCF or Black Campus Ministries staffworker.
- ☐ your own IVCF staffworker or the outreach ministry of your church.
- ☐ a former church member or alumnus from your chapter who is working as a missionary.

■ *Guidelines for leading an international study* by Tom Sirinides. Your group is likely to have a wonderfully diverse mix of people from many different backgrounds. These guidelines were created for leaders of the Rutgers International Christian Fellowship to help them understand the unique needs of the group.

1. Gear the language and pace of the discussion to those who

are unfamiliar with the Bible, with English or with both. Avoid the use of Christian terms and jargon whenever possible. If others in the group use them, pause to make a general explanation of the term.

2. After the passage has been read, ask if there are any questions about words, and offer definitions as necessary.

3. Watch for a confused or puzzled look on the face of a group member. Ask them if they have a question. They may be totally lost, or only slightly confused, but in either case the anxiety of the situation can make it hard to think—especially in a foreign language (which English is to many in our group).

4. Try to be aware, as well, when a quieter member seems to be thinking, or starts to speak but is unwittingly cut off by a more vocal member of the group. People are often struggling to formulate their thoughts (again, an especially difficult thing to do in a foreign language), and unless someone such as you, the leader, pauses the flow of the discussion on their behalf, their thoughts may not come together fully until after the conversation has already moved on. Just saying, "Bill, did you want to say something?" can be enough to facilitate this process.

5. Some application questions are not suitable for a group such as ours, with many non-Christians. In preparing and leading, it is helpful to seek an application that is of relevance to both Christians and non-Christians alike. Use this as the study's conclusion. Christians and non-Christians have many common concerns (strength to deal with hardship, peace in the midst of stress and pressure, hope for the future), and so an application of this type will be meaningful to a broader audience than one about altering your prayer life or witnessing more fervently, for example. These things are important, but not always suitable for our group. Our goal is that everyone would see the relevance of the Bible to their own life today, whether they are Christians yet or not.

6. Also regarding application questions: Using the approach of "Here's something to think about" can work well in a group with non-Christians, and especially with many East Asians. ("Saving face" is very important in most cultures of East Asia.) People can

feel threatened by a request to verbally discuss their failings and sins in a group setting. But a "thought question" causes people to consider the relevance of the passage to their lives without forcing them to disclose it publicly. Rather than putting the pressure on members to "open up" (which can distract people from the question and focus them on their fears), a thought question both frees them to respond to the study and leaves the door open for meaningful one-to-one conversations afterward.

7. Remember: You as the leader are the "guardian" of the discussion. Try to see that there is fairly balanced participation in the study. Don't let a few members (usually those who are quite familiar with English and/or with the Bible) dominate things or move the discussion along too quickly. Don't let other group members (often those who are fairly new to English and/or to the Bible) feel left out. Encourage the more talkative members to hold back, and seek to draw out the quieter ones.

8. Depending on the international student(s), they may or may not feel comfortable with verbal prayer. (Some appreciate being prayed for regardless.) One student from Taiwan found that the prayer time forced her to deal with the battle she was feeling. "Pray for me because Buddha doesn't want me to believe this," she said. She later became a Christian. (Jane Pelz, Ill.)

9. Above all, ask God for wisdom and guidance as you lead. He has promised to provide it for us if we ask him.

■ *Reaching out to internationals.* People who are new to a country will greatly appreciate your friendship and help in making the transition and understanding the culture. Any university campus is likely to have international students, and many metropolitan areas will also have people who are new to the country. Refugee placement centers may be able to give you names of international people with particular needs (Contact World Relief, P.O. Box WRC, Wheaton, IL 60187 [708] 665-0235) as well as university admissions centers.

☐ To develop vision for reaching international people, study Genesis together. This will help you better understand the Abrahamic covenant and God's plan for the whole world of using the Jews to call the Gentiles to himself. (Jane Pelz)

- ☐ Help internationals adjust to our culture and experience your city: meet them at the airport, help them move into dorms or apartments, show them around the university, show them around the city, hold socials to which you can invite them, invite them home for weekends or holidays.
- ☐ Plan special events such as a joint InterVarsity/International Student Club get-together. (Jane Pelz)
- ☐ Pray weekly for international friends.
- ☐ Invite Christian international students to join your small group. (Jane Pelz)
- ☐ Attend the international club or another ethnic club. (Jane Pelz)
- ☐ Plan a worship service with a church of a different ethnic group. You will learn from one another's worship traditions and strengths. Many members may be recent immigrants or people who are still learning English. Keep in mind, however, that there may also be a second or third generation of people in the church who were born in the U.S. and are completely acclimated to the culture.
- ☐ Lead an international Bible study geared toward non-Christians and/or people who are still learning English. Begin by inviting some friends or acquaintances over and ask them if they would be interested in studying the Bible together. Meet in a reserved room in the library, an empty classroom or a dorm room. (Jane Pelz)

  ■ Watch cartoons together. Cartoons have simplified language for those who are still learning, and cartoons about the Bible are a launching point for Bible study. The Family Entertainment Network cartoons deal with the stories of the Old Testament and some of the Gospel stories. The cartoons bring to life Jesus and his teachings, and it is much easier for the group to discuss the passage. The Superbook Cartoon about Adam and Eve can be used to study the first three chapters in Genesis. This cuts down the time spent in explaining the various English words in the Bible that are not familiar and allows for more time to interact. (Will and Vittoria Grant, D.C.)

☐ Nairy Ohanian suggests an activity for international students called "Around the World." It allows the students to reconnect with home and share history, and serves as a springboard for missions prayer! Bring 8″ × 15″ paper (if possible) and colored markers and have each group member draw a world map as best as they can or bring photocopies of world maps. On their maps have them locate where they were born, where their family now lives, one country they have visited, one country they want to visit in the future and one country which they would like to pray for and why. Share drawings with the group; then pray for the countries indicated for prayer. Pray for families too, if time permits. Encourage group members to take their maps home and use them to continue praying for missions.

■ *Read a missionary biography.* All group members can read and discuss a book, or one group member can read and report back. William Carey Library (P.O. Box 40129, Pasadena, CA 91114) and STL Books (Box 28, Waynesboro, GA 30830) are good sources of missionary biographies. Write for a catalog.

■ *Short-term missions.* Some agencies (including IVCF Global Projects and STIM) will take your whole group as a team. Personal and group development from such an experience is tremendous. If it is not possible to go as a whole group, you can send one small group member. Here are some ways to support that person.

☐ Pray for the spiritual, physical and emotional preparation of your member. Pray also for the people with whom and to whom she or he will be going.

☐ Help in fundraising.

☐ Help address, stuff and mail prayer letters.

☐ Go shopping for items needed for the trip.

☐ Do research on the country and people your friend will be serving.

☐ Make and eat meals together that will be similar to the food your member will be eating.

☐ Buy gifts that your member can give during the trip.

☐ Make a journal for the member to read at intervals throughout the short-term. Have each member write an encouraging note and put a date to be read on it.

- ☐ Plan a going-away party and/or packing party.
- ☐ See your member off at the airport.
- ☐ Assign weeks throughout the short-term for members to write to the short-termer.
- ☐ Meet the short-termer at the airport upon return.
- ☐ Be patient and provide opportunity for your friend to talk about their time away. Help him or her focus by asking questions.
- ☐ Encourage the short-termer to take time to readjust to life here.
- ☐ Pray with your friend about people he or she met, the ministry that went on, for continuance in the ministry, for an understanding of next steps.

■ *Sponsor a missionary* by Brian Hossink. Get the name of a missionary from your denomination or your staff worker. Pray regularly for the missionary, take a donation (or do a fundraiser like collecting soda cans and returning them for cash), read letters from the missionary and pray about specific requests, and send letters weekly to let your missionary know that they are being prayed for. Send birthday cards and care packages of items they need. Send newspaper articles about trends and important events to keep them informed of life back home. If it's available to you and the missionary, e-mail is the best way to keep in touch with people overseas.

Social awareness and action

■ *Defining justice* by Jana Webb. Read Amos 2:6-7; 4:1-2; 5:11; 6:4-7; 8:4-6; 9:8. From these verses how would you define our call to the ministry of justice? Pray together for hearts of justice. Read Matthew 25:31-46. Who are the hungry, thirsty, strangers, naked and prisoners in your community? How can you minister to their needs? (Adapted from *Economic Justice,* a Global Issues Bible Study [Downers Grove, Ill.: InterVarsity Press], 1990.)

■ *Environmental stewardship* by Ruth Goring. Here are a few ideas which will help you to be more aware of God's creation. You can do them as a group or on your own with follow-up discussion.

- ☐ Take a hike or stroll through a park. Sit down on the grass or on a rock and contemplate your surroundings—the variegations in a rock, the patterns of tree bark, the veins of a leaf. Think of the pleasure God took in creating these things.
- ☐ Take a walk and pick up litter as you go or find a vacant lot that needs some cleanup and go to it.
- ☐ Contact a local biologist or conservation group and find out whether any plant or animal species in your area is endangered because of human activity and what you can do about it.
- ☐ Read Genesis 1:1—2:25 and make a list of what the passage teaches regarding the relationship between human beings and the rest of the created order.
- ☐ Keep track of your car's mileage and have it checked for polluting emissions. Can you use less gas by taking the bus, riding a bike, carpooling or walking?
- ☐ Read aloud Psalm 96 and spend time worshiping God for his generous sustenance of his creatures.
- ☐ Buy organically grown food and/or talk to your grocer about your desire to have organically grown produce.
- ☐ Do a bit of gardening. If you don't have a place to plant, find out about renting space (usually very cheap) in a public space. Or if someone in the small group has the land, work on a garden together. If your church has enough land, consider establishing a community garden and invite others from the church and neighborhoods to come and take a plot.
- ☐ Read Hosea 4:1-3 and discuss the relationship between our treatment of one another and our harmony with the land.
- ☐ Begin composting vegetable wastes (rinds, pulp, eggshells, seeds). Simply bury your wastes in your gardening area, or deliver them regularly to someone who gardens.
- ☐ Talk to a Christian farmer about the issues he or she faces in working the land lovingly.
- ☐ Solicitation letters and other junk mailings are often printed on only one side of a sheet of paper. Save these sheets and use them for notes and memos. When both sides have been used—recycle.

for notes and memos. When both sides have been used—recycle.

☐ Water—so ordinary, so taken for granted—is a wonderful gift from God. Examine your water-use habits. Perhaps you can take shorter showers. Dishwashers use much more water and electricity than hand-washing. A commercial car wash is likewise much more extravagant than bucket-and-rag-style washing. How can you save water?

☐ Often people from Two-Thirds World countries can help us see what is wasteful about our lifestyle. Talk to an international person about these issues and find out what ideas he or she has.

☐ Plan an Earthkeeping Day for your fellowship, campus, church or community. Talk about what God has been unfolding for you about our responsibilities toward the earth, and offer resources to help others begin to practice an earthkeeping ethic.

☐ Read a book about environmental stewardship, such as *Earthkeeping*, edited by Loren Wilkinson (Grand Rapids, Mich.: Eerdmans, 1980), or *Redeeming Creation* by Fred C. Van Dyke et al. (Downers Grove, Ill.: InterVarsity Press, 1996).

☐ Get involved with organizations which promote environmental concerns, such as Co-Op America (2100 M St., NW, Suite 310, Washington, D.C. 20063 [202] 872-5307), Eco-Justice Working Group (475 Riverside Dr., New York, NY 10115 [202] 872-5307), Greenpeace (1436 U St. NW, Washington, D.C. 20009 [202] 462-1177), National Wildlife Federation (1400 16th St. NW, Washington, D.C. 20036 [202] 797-6800) or Sierra Club (730 Polk St., San Francisco, CA 94109 [415] 776-2211).

☐ Read Colossians 1:9-14 aloud as your prayer. Thank God that Jesus has mended your broken relationship with nature, and ask him for love and wisdom to live out that reconciliation.

(Adapted from *Environmental Stewardship*, a Global Issues Bible Study [Downers Grove, Ill.: InterVarsity Press], 1990.)

■ *Global Issues Bible Studies*. Edited by Stephen Hayner and Gordon Aeschliman and authored by experts in each field, this series helps us understand the problems confronting our world, shows us how God responds to people in need and encourages us to inductive studies in each of these guides: *Basic Human Needs, Economic Justice, Fundamentalistic Religion, Healing for Broken People, Leadership in the 21st Century, Multi-Ethnicity, People and Technology, Sanctity of Life, Spiritual Conflict, Urbanization* and *Voiceless People.*

■ *Habitat for Humanity* by Brian Hossink. Volunteer one Saturday or on a regular basis to help build homes with Habitat for Humanity (419 W. Church St., Americus, GA 31709 [912] 924-6135). They can use people with a variety of skill levels—or no skills!

■ *Join Evangelicals for Social Action.* This organization, founded by Ron Sider, promotes peace and justice in public life. It has local chapters and a magazine, *Prism.* Write to them at 10 Lancaster Ave., Philadelphia, PA 19151 or call (215) 645-9390.

■ *Nursing home visits* by University of Illinois Staff. Prepare and share a worship service at a nursing home.

■ *Racial reconciliation* by Brian Hossink. If your group is homogenous and you want to connect with people of other ethnicities, invite a Christian group or church of a different ethnic background to join you at your meetings. Attend their meetings. Cosponsor activities. This will allow you to build community and learn from one another.

■ *Serve the homeless* by Brian Hossink. Go together to work at a local mission, shelter or soup kitchen. Get together and bake goods to send to a shelter or soup kitchen.

■ *Sponsor a child.* For a very small amount of money (perhaps twenty dollars a month) your group can take care of the physical needs of a child in a developing country. The agency will send you pictures and information so that you can write to the child and pray for him or her. Contact Compassion International, 3955 Cragwood Drive, Colorado Springs, CO 80933 or World Vision, 919 West Huntington Drive, Monrovia, CA 91016.

■ *The Tightwad Gazette.* As a group, subscribe to the newsletter or purchase one of the collected volumes of ideas (more ideas for your money) published by Villard Books. Talk about how you can live more cheaply in light of the needs of others and environmental stewardship. Make plans to give away the money you save. For a sample newsletter send a self-addressed, stamped, business-sized envelope to *The Tightwad Gazette,* RR1 Box 3570, Leeds, ME 04263.

■ *Voiceless people* by Chuck Shelton. People without voices are powerless and cannot speak for themselves. Their needs go unmet and they suffer. They are the handicapped, the poor, abused women and children, the frail elderly, the unborn, the homeless, the hungry, the illiterate, the unemployed and people of color. To focus on the needs of the voiceless read Isaiah 61:1-4. List ten actions to be taken by a person the Spirit of the Lord rests on. Beside each of these actions list an example of what living it out would be like in your community, church, family or campus. For example, working on a Habitat for Humanity project to build housing with the poor would "repair the ruined city." Select one of these actions and make plans to start doing it this week. (Adapted from *Voiceless People,* a Global Issues Bible Study [Downers Grove, Ill.: InterVarsity Press], 1990.)

■ *A world awareness week.*

☐ Conduct studies on world hunger.

☐ Bring in speakers on specific topics like energy use.

☐ Encourage one another in lifestyle changes.

☐ Support Bread for the World (802 Rhode Island Ave. N.E., Washington, D.C. 20018) or Food for the Hungry (7729 E. Greenway Road, Scottsdale, AZ 85260) or other groups which raise money to feed hungry people.

☐ Plan a hunger or world awareness meal for your church or fellowship.

☐ Use one day of the week for fasting and prayer for the world. (See section on *Prayer fast* in chapter two.)

☐ Contact one of the following organizations for further ideas: Lutheran World Relief, 360 Park Avenue South, New York, NY 10010 (212) 532-6350; Mercy Corps International, 3030 SW First Avenue, Portland, OR 97201 (503) 242-1032; World Concern, 19303 Fremont Ave. North, Seattle, WA 98133 (206) 546-7201.

■ *Write.* Letters to congressional representatives and other political officials on issues such as world hunger or energy.

Books on Outreach

Bakke, Raymond. *The Urban Christian.* Downers Grove, Ill.: InterVarsity Press, 1983. An excellent tool for those considering ministry in an urban setting. Bakke gives a brief theology of the city and tells of his own experiences and strategies.

Campolo, Tony, and Gordon Aeschliman. *Fifty Ways You Can Feed a Hungry World.* Downers Grove, Ill: InterVarsity Press, 1991. Practical and manageable ideas for helping others that you can do with your group.

Campolo, Tony, and Gordon Aeschliman. *Fifty Ways You Can Share Your Faith.* Downers Grove, Ill.: InterVarsity Press, 1992. Simple ideas for reaching people with the gospel.

Dawson, John. *Taking Our Cities for God.* Altamonte Springs, Fla.: Creation House, 1989. How we can pray for our cities.

Elmer, Duane. *Cross-Cultural Conflict.* Downers Grove, Ill.: InterVarsity Press, 1993. Each culture has a unique way of handling conflict; understanding the distinctives of cultural groups helps grow relationships. This book will introduce you to these dynamics.

Harrison, Dan, and Gordon Aeschliman. *Romancing the Globe.* Downers Grove, Ill.: InterVarsity Press, 1993. An introduction to how twentysomethings can be involved in world mission.

Johnstone, Patrick. *Operation World,* fifth edition. Grand Rapids, Mich.: Zondervan, 1993. A daily guide to praying for the world with facts about missions in every part of the world.

Knechtle, Cliff. *Give Me an Answer.* Downers Grove, Ill.: InterVarsity Press, 1986. A seasoned evangelist gives answers to the questions seekers most frequently ask.

Lau, Lawson. *The World at Your Doorstep.* Downers Grove, Ill.: InterVarsity Press, 1984. A brief guide to short-term missions.

Little, Paul. *How to Give Away Your Faith,* revised. Downers Grove, Ill.: InterVarsity Press, 1988. Encouragment for those who are uncertain about how to share the gospel.

Little, Paul. *Know Why You Believe.* Downers Grove, Ill.: InterVarsity Press, 1988. Help in answering the hard questions you or others have about Christianity.

Malcom, Kari Torjesen. *We Signed Away Our Lives.* Downers Grove, Ill.: InterVarsity Press, 1990. The story of a missionary family in China.

Perkins, Spencer, and Chris Rice. *More Than Equals.* Downers Grove, Ill.: InterVarsity Press, 1993. Account of a friendship between a white man and an African-American man that changed their perception of race relationships.

Pippert, Rebecca Manley. *Out of the Saltshaker.* Downers Grove, Ill.: InterVarsity Press, 1979. Classic call to evangelism by a former IVCF staffworker with many motivating and inspiring stories.

Scazzero, Peter. *Introducing Jesus.* Downers Grove, Ill.: InterVarsity Press, 1991. A brief book that explains how to start an investigative Bible discussion group for seekers. Six Bible studies which can be photocopied for the group are included.

Sider, Ronald J. *Rich Christians in an Age of Hunger.* Waco, Tex.: Word, 1990. A challenge to use material resources well in light of the needs of those around you and of the whole world.

Sire, James. *Jesus, the Reason.* A LifeGuide® Bible Study. Downers Grove, Ill.: InterVarsity Press, 1996. Eleven studies on who Jesus is and why he is the basis of our faith. Great for seekers.

Stiles, J. Mack. *Speaking of Jesus.* Downers Grove, Ill.: InterVarsity Press, 1995. An inspiring and practical book on sharing the gospel with friends.